FOOTNOTES TO A THEOLOGY

The Karl Barth Colloquium of 1972

edited and with an Introduction by

MARTIN RUMSCHEIDT

 SUPPLEMENTS

FOOTNOTES TO A THEOLOGY

The Karl Barth Colloquium of 1972

edited and with an Introduction by

H. MARTIN RUMSCHEIDT

WIPF & STOCK · Eugene, Oregon

Wipf and Stock Publishers
199 W 8th Ave, Suite 3
Eugene, OR 97401

Footnotes to a Theology
The Karl Barth Colloquium of 1972
By Rumscheidt, H. Martin
Copyright © 1974 CCSR All rights reserved.
Softcover ISBN-13: 978-1-7252-6810-4
Hardcover ISBN-13: 978-1-7252-6812-8
eBook ISBN-13: 978-1-7252-6811-1
Publication date 2/25/2020
Previously published by Ontario: CSR, 1974

FOREWORD

The essays which are brought together here were originally delivered during the first colloquium of the Karl Barth Society of North America. It met at Victoria University in Toronto on October 26 to 28, 1972, and was entitled: The Theology of Karl Barth. The addresses by Markus Barth and Arthur Cochrane were given during the Colloquium Dinner; the others were more 'formal' and followed by at times very animated discussion.

During that colloquium the Karl Barth Society of North America was inaugurated. Its aim, far from being a personality-cult of Karl Barth, is to encourage a critical and constructive theology through the exploration of his work. It is envisaged that the assistance given to the Karl Barth Stiftung in Europe in its purpose to collect and preserve all literature by and about Karl Barth, the publication of a complete edition of his works together with the establishment on this Continent of a similar collection will make available for theological research materials that will adequately meet the proposed aim. Both the academic and the pastoral areas of theology are meant to benefit from the endeavours of this Society.

It is quite apparent that the aims of the Barth Society and of the Corporation for the Publication of Academic Studies in Religion in Canada overlap at certain points. The latter was founded with the specified purpose of "publishing a journal and other materials to serve the needs of scholars working in both the French and English languages in Canada in all fields of the academic study of religion". The Corporation is, therefore, pleased, that the directors of the Karl Barth Society have asked us to publish this collection of addresses. This volume is a part of those "other materials" referred to above: it is, indeed, a supplementary volume to the journal SR: Studies in Religion/Sciences Religieuses, published by this Corporation.

As I am 'wearing a director's cap' both of the Karl Barth Society and of this Corporation I am doubly pleased in the publication of this volume. As director of the former I thank my fellow board members for their readiness to have these addresses published by the Corporation, as president of the latter I thank my fellow directors of its board for accepting them as a supplement volume to our journal. With appreciation and pleasure I add an expression of thanks to those Canadian universities, religion departments and theological schools and colleges,

FOREWORD

members of which belong sometimes to both this Corporation and the Barth Society, for their donations to the Corporation in support of its aims, for it was that assistance which has made thinking seriously about publications supplementing SR possible.

>Martin Rumscheidt
>President
>The Corporation for the Publication
>of Academic Studies in Religion in
>Canada.

Contents

Foreword   v

Introduction   H. MARTIN RUMSCHEIDT   1

Barth's Commentary on the Romans, 1922-1972, or
Karl Barth vs. the Exegetes   PAUL S. MINEAR   8

Philosophy and Theology - A Family Affair (Karl
and Heinrich Barth)   JOSEPH C. McLELLAND   30

The Concreteness of Theology: Reflections on the
Conversation between Barth and Bonhoeffer
                                 PAUL L. LEHMANN   53

Current Discussions on the Political Character
of Karl Barth's Theology   MARKUS BARTH   77

Why was and is the Theology of Karl Barth
of Interest to a Jewish Theologian?
                                 MICHAEL WYSCHOGROD   95

The Impact of Karl Barth on the Catholic Church
in the last half Century   EMILIEN LAMIRANDE   112

The Karl Barth I Knew   ARTHUR C. COCHRANE   142

The Contributors   149

H. MARTIN RUMSCHEIDT

Introduction

'Footnotes to a Theology' - what an ambiguous title for a publication of addresses delivered to a society whose aim is said to exclude the veneration of him whose name it bears. The Karl Barth Society of North America really does not want to 'footnote' the 'master's' theology.
 A negative declaration of intent does not, however, help to explain the title of this volume. The explanation must begin with the assertion that the title refers to the addresses collected here and not to the Society. What it wants to do has already been stated: encourage critical and constructive theology through exploration of Barth's work. It is clear to its members that he left a legacy to the Church and to the community of scholars whose work is the study of theology and of religion. That this legacy does not have to be taken seriously simply because it is Karl Barth's is also clear, just as much as that it cannot be ignored. But there will be a parting of minds over why the exploration of his work is fruitful for critical and constructive theology today. There are those who believe that the attention Barth's work demands is due to "the fact that for him priority in the process of theological understanding lay exclusively and all-pervadingly on the Word of God in Christ, who makes his Word heard to those who, through the Holy Spirit, are attentive to the Scriptures."[1] This concentration on the Word as object of theology is regarded here as a passion for objectivity; Barth's unrelenting circling around the Word manifests the pathos of an objective scientist. Factors as these are held up as reasons why his work not only calls for but indeed deserves serious attention. To others Barth's attractiveness lies more in his critical iconoclasm or in his insistence that all theological assertions are parabolic or analogical in nature and are not immediately or directly representative of the truth theological understanding seeks to grasp. Such people can take Barth seriously without accepting his assertion that the Word is the determinative object of the theological endeavour or without agreeing to the individual conclusions to which Barth came on his own critical and constructive road. "Either we must enter

INTRODUCTION

with him into a vision of the unlimited sovereignty of God's grace that reduces all else to negativity, finding this vision as the uniform message of the Bible, or we are forced simply to confess that this vision is not real for us and that we must stand outside the circle of faith defined by it. Few men in our age or any age have come so near in confronting us with a final choice for or against faith. If Barth has failed, as I believe he has, his has been one of the most brilliant failures of all times."[2] Yet such 'outsiders', as the author of this quotation would consider himself, do see the need to take Barth seriously. Thus, to speak of 'footnotes to a theology' is, indeed, not to describe the outlook of the membership nor to define the aims of the Karl Barth Society of North America. The Society surely ought to include 'right' and 'left' wing Barth interpreters.

The authors of these addresses do not conceal the fact that the man Karl Barth attracted them and that his work did have an impact on theirs. Whether a son would say that his relationship to his father is defined by the latter's winsome personality and powers of thought is left unexplored, precisely because Markus Barth refrained more than the others from such autobiographical comments or even indirect hints. All warned against 'footnoting'. There really can be no mere explaining of the theology of Karl Barth, because neither such explaining nor that theology is an end in itself. If the editor nevertheless chooses that title he wishes to underscore the implicitly held view that illumining Barth's work and influence is one way of moving with him and beyond him in the interest of a critical and constructive theology for our times.

It is not necessarily self-evident that a variety of addresses as the seven in this volume do have a common focus or intent other than that which the title of the Colloquium itself suggested: the theology of Karl Barth. But that is no focus at all, unless one is prepared to speak similarly of the whole side of a barn as a target for precision-shooting. Yet all the way from Minear's _Barth vs. the Exegetes_ to Lamirande's _The Impact of Barth on the Catholic Church_, from McLelland's _Family Affair_ to Cochrane's _The Barth I Knew_ there is this conviction: the theology of Karl Barth is of interest because of the sort of questions he raised. "What are

INTRODUCTION

the prospects of Christianity today? What has it to say today and tomorrow in face and in the midst of the cataclysmic changes in which humanity is engulfed? How is Christianity to hold its own in competition with and under the assault of newly arisen political religions and reinvigorated older religions? How is it to fulfil its mission in the technical world of the future? What is Christianity, the Gospel, Christian faith? In Barth's writing there is no practicable prescription for answering these questions. He is not indeed the only one to face them and to say important things regarding them."[3] We, too, must face them, in fact, how could we fail to do so anyway? The interest which the authors of the addresses show in Barth's work is evidently nourished more by the resoluteness and sustaining power of the way he faces those and other questions than exclusively by his answers to them. And yet one cannot deny that that resoluteness and sustaining power do account for the fact that many of Barth's answers are not only important in the eyes of many but also right.

Paul Minear illuminates the rather curious lack of dialogue between Barth's 'commentary' on Romans and nearly the entire guild of St. Paul's recent exegetes. Is there too deep a hiatus between the technical, scientific exegesis of Scripture and the theological one? Is Harnack right when he insists that the theological professorship must not be confused with the pulpit ministry?[4] Of course, Barth had dethroned the gods of the seminar-rooms, as Minear puts it, the gods of Minear's own guild. That may very well have been an iconoclastic stroke, but was it constructive for the task at hand - the understanding of a man of ancient times? Paul Minear states that it was, because it shook the understanding of time, of temporality, and of history loose from the insufficient, two-dimensional view held by these scholars and called attention to a sense of time in St. Paul's writing with which not only Barth, but in his quite different way also Bultmann, and more recently such literary figures as G. Poulet and A. Mendilow were struggling. Minear does not subscribe to Barth's own proposed solution to that problem of time, but then that is not the point. At issue here is rather the realization that Barth's bombshell on the theologians' playground prevents those who are playing there now from losing track of time, especially their own.

INTRODUCTION

Any modern-day Tertullian might well ask: what does Karl have to do with Heinrich? substituting personal for geographical names. Joseph McLelland, who is certainly no Tertullian, speaks of a family affair in trying to answer that question. His essay shows that the two brothers, who both held chairs at the same university, owed much to each other in their understanding of and approaches to the other's discipline. Apparently neither removed the insignia of his guild before engaging the other. What would that suggest about the much argued problem: Karl Barth and philosophy? It remains an impossible dream to show that Karl Barth was, after all, 'really' open to philosophy. What becomes clear in McLelland's address is the Barthian dilemma - to insist on the ancillary position of philosophy in the exercise of theology but yet to make cheerful use of philosophy in its critical, epistemological task. But can one ask that seriously of philosophy? This question, raised by McLelland, is illumined by the family affair. He reveals the Kantian underground, the 'synthetic a priori' in both men's views of their respective and each other's disciplines. And that loads the definitions of philosophy and theology unduly in one direction. Is the Kantian understanding the only one? Of course not, but it is the one Barth works with and which he places in opposition to theology as 'the most beautiful of all sciences'. The dialogue of these opposites in Barth's work is ambiguous, yes self-deceiving, concludes McLelland. But it does move theology, at times also Barth's, to what is called limiting concepts where there arise better perspectives on the relation of philosophy and theology as well as a <u>Mitmenschlichkeit</u> of their representatives in terms of humour.

Thomas Mendip's declamation "O tedium, tedium, tedium... Where in this small talking world can I find a longitude with no platitude" leads to the centre of Paul Lehmann's search for concreteness in theology. In his own words, why is our theological existence today devoid of persuasive and freeing concreteness and vulnerable to idolatrous and cultic concreteness filling the vacuum in our theological discrimination? Clearly there is today a preoccupation with concreteness in theology and it is just as earnest as was Barth's and Bonhoeffer's. Yet exactly the preoccupation of these men brings the current search for concreteness to a critical juncture, for they

INTRODUCTION

are being asked now to show how to make sense of Jesus Christ in the midst of a culture and experience of the world come of age, whereas they ask theologians now to make sense of the culture and experience of that world come of age with due regard to the concrete pressure and presence of Jesus Christ in our midst. Lehmann's discerning discussion of the Barth-Bonhoeffer relationship sheds much light on the history of recent theology and that alone is worthy of 'footnoting'. But his motive and goal are something different; it is the urgency of a theological existence today at our concrete place where we are called to be, or in different words, it is the unavoidable necessity of the search for a faith for being human in the similarly unavoidably necessary struggle against the mounting arrogance and brutality of power. Such a faith comes as a consequence of concreteness in theology and would indeed be a longitude without platitudes.

Markus Barth's address is a report on a very vigorous debate about what really matters in Karl Barth's theology. The lines of the protagonists are clearly drawn so that one may well speak, as in the case of Hegel's followers, of right-wing and left-wing Barthians. To the one the determinative object is the subject of Jesus Christ, the revelation of God to man and it is the progressive penetration into the mystery of Jesus Christ, so obvious in Barth's thought, which warrants that conviction. To the others Barth's discovery of God's revolution and its acme - the resurrection of the dead and the establishment of God's kingdom on earth - precedes the discovery of Christ's centrality. Christology, however necessary a feature for Barth, does not replace what is essential for him: God and the proletariat. A debate like that cannot really be called a 'footnote to a theology'. On the other hand the label does apply because in that debate there lurks much the question of the practical task of Christian theology: what is the proclamation of Jesus Christ, or what is discipleship?

Michael Wyschogrod had introduced the phrase: why is the theology of Karl Barth of interest? For him it was a matter of discerning why Barth is of interest to a Jewish theologian. His answers were not meant to commend Barth to all theologians. But Wyschogrod believes himself to be in the presence of a member of the family simply because Barth is so scriptural, so humbled by the largely

INTRODUCTION

Jewish Word of God, which Wyschogrod paraphrases as the witness to a movement of God toward man. One reads in his address that Barth, unlike Bultmann, is no gentile, one in whose theology some alien frame of reference, such as alleged verities of reason, can prescribe or even anticipate God's decisions. If he is no gentile then what is Barth? He is a Christian, says Wyschogrod, someone who, even though a member of the family, differs because his faith regarding the free and sovereign act of the God of Israel is different from that of the Jewish member of the family. Wyschogrod can best illuminate that difference with the suggestion that in some respects Judaism is more Barthian than Barth! What a footnote that is! But Michael Wyschogrod tempers his appreciation with some stinging criticism. He cites a lengthy enumeration of the attributes Barth applies to the synagogue. Here the spectre of anti-semitism arises and that, to say the least, has become one of the thorniest problems of theology and theological existence today. To be constructive in our time, the thought and existence of the theologian must overcome a past in which it was not only possible to ignore Jews but, indeed, to do away with them on the ground of arguments theologically 'justified'.

   The next address, that of Emilien Lamirande, offers a comprehensive picture of how those, whom Barth on the whole regarded as the more alert critics of his work, responded to it. But then it is often quite helpful to discern the accents of someone's thought by looking at the way the protagonists <u>sich auseinandersetzen</u>. (Cassell's <u>Dictionary</u> renders that as 'coming to terms with'.) But since it is a fact that as soon as someone has spoken a word he can no longer claim sole possession of and jurisdiction over it but must now let it subject itself to the understanding of his hearers, attention to such <u>Auseinandersetzungen</u> itself is part of the process of understanding, of critique and of being timely.

   The focus of only one of the addresses gathered in this volume, Arthur Cochrane's, is Karl Barth the man rather than his theology. Yet Cochrane wisely warns at the end of his warm appreciation of the man Karl Barth that devotion to theologians must never take the place of concentration on the truth theology seeks to grasp. For this warning, Cochrane cites Karl Barth himself as his 'authority' - it is a source of great amusement to the angels when men try so hard to 'footnote' other theologians

INTRODUCTION

instead of becoming wounded, like Jacob, in wrestling with the God who is with men.

All of these essays, attempts to understand Karl Barth, seek to further the much more daring attempt, namely man's speech concerning God. That this attempt will go on, critically, constructively and with real <u>Mitmenschlichkeit</u>, namely with humour, is the wish of this volume and of the Karl Barth Society.

NOTES

1 Heinrich Vogel, <u>Freundschaft mit Karl Barth</u>, Zürich, T.V.Z. Verlag, 1973, p. 68
2 John B. Cobb, Jr., <u>Living Options in Protestant Theology</u>, Philadelphia, Westminster Press, 1962, p. 197
3 Karl Barth, <u>Church Dogmatics</u>, ed. by Helmut Gollwitzer, New York, Harper and Row, 1962, p. 2f
4 Martin Rumscheidt, <u>Revelation and Theology-An Analysis of the Barth-Harnack Correspondence of 1923</u>, London, Cambridge University Press, 1972, p. 36

PAUL S. MINEAR

Barth's Commentary On The Romans, 1922-1972;
Or Karl Barth Vs. The Exegetes

During the past five decades the cleavage between the biblical and the theological disciplines has steadily widened, in accordance with the curricular demands of highly departmentalized universities. Few historians attempt the theological task; few dogmaticians attempt the exegetical. Not so Barth. Seldom has a theologian so fully immersed himself in the historical problems, wrestling responsibly with the endless hermeneutical challenges posed by the Scriptures. Each single volume of the Dogmatics has more sustained exegesis, usually in the fine print, than do most volumes produced by biblical historians. Yet biblical scholars have either ignored or deplored this cultivation of their own domain. Why? We may find an answer by exploring the early stages of the encounter and then examining the situation near the end of the half century.

In spite of an abundance of first-hand sources, it is difficult to recapture the barometric pressures prevalent during the early stages of the conflict, between 1915 and 1925. Efforts to recover those pressures remind us of how anachronistic historical work is bound to be. For one thing, our interest in that early decade is a product of later developments, and we cannot erase knowledge of them from our minds in our effort to turn the clock back. Even the phrase "the early Barth" guarantees a distortion in the portrait by reflecting later history. The man himself recognized this. As early as 1932 he wrote, "When I look back at the book (Romans) it seems to have been written by another man to meet a situation belonging to a past epoch."[1]

It was the change in his vocational situation which, among other things, made Barth himself the first post-Barthian. In 1932 he was a professor of theology. In 1918 he had been an individual Christian pastor, who had suddenly uncovered a strange world in the Bible where God had spoken to him with compelling authority. As most of us know, there is a vast difference between reading the Bible as a person crying out for divine help and studying it as a professor. Few of us can measure that distance because our own encounters with the Bible have for so long been oriented toward meeting professional demands. Yet there is a difference. Failure to recognize it is one of the few defects in Brevard S. Childs' <u>The Crisis of Biblical Theology</u>. Childs treats the various leaders in the early biblical theology movement as if they wanted "to form a school or devise a system"[2] whereas it was actually the initiative of the Bible in answering their cries for deliverance which forced them off the treadmill of system-building. The power of this initiative is neglected when the movement is characterized simply as a shift in the mode of biblical studies.[3] Let us remember that Barth's <u>Commentary</u> was primarily the work of a young pastor, seeking to meet the needs of his parish.

We also should remember the familiar but frequently ignored fact that history, though written backward, is lived forward. Facing the unknown future at the point of decision-making involves a different perception of the temporal process than when a person looks back at known decisions and known results. Looking back at Barth's <u>Commentary</u> we activate a sense of time different from that which was released in Barth as he read the Epistle of Paul. The same fifty years means to the earlier author something different than to the later historian. Retrospect does change things. Some of us, in looking back, are tempted to glorify that earlier situation, building the tomb of this particular prophet, in spite of the profound warning of Jesus against such tomb-building (Mt.23:29f.). Others are tempted to exaggerate the distance we have traveled since Barth, thus making a desperate effort to keep up-to-date or even to reach the future ahead of time. Many scholars have celebrated the beginning of the post-Barthian epoch, beginning as early as 1928 when a German journal announced that Barth "is already slipping into the position of a man of yesterday". To this, Barth replied: "Dead men ride fast but successful theologians ride faster". (<u>Commentary</u>, p.26)

This difference in time perspectives is even more acute when the modern historian deals with the apostle Paul. Imbedded in historical methodology is a sense of time foreign to Paul. Of this collision Barth became aware in his reading of the Epistle to the Romans. In fact, it was his effort to do justice to Paul's consciousness of time that alienated professional exegetes. Where Barth was willing to adapt his perception of time in order to grasp Paul's message, his exegetical colleagues were unwilling to do so.

The early stages in this development come clear in the correspondence of Barth with Eduard Thurneysen, so usefully made available by James D. Smart: <u>Revolutionary Theology in the Making</u>. Barth and Thurneysen had first met as students, studying under Wilhelm Herrmann at Marburg; then they had become pastors of churches in neighboring Swiss villages, Safenwil and Leutwil. Soon after they began their pastorates, the First World War broke out, involving the universities in which they had been studying. Their revered theological mentors joined voluntarily in public declarations of support for the Kaiser, a support which shocked the young pastors.[4] To them it indicated a pollution of Protestantism by nationalism and secularism. As Barth wrote to his friend on Oct. 15, 1915: "Everything that has to do with the state is taken a hundred times more seriously than God."[5] They recognized that the very word God, as used so glibly by the churches, had lost its meaning; this God had died.[6] And of his theological teachers, Barth wrote: "I suddenly realized that I could not any longer follow either their ethics and dogmatics, or their understanding of the Bible and history."[7] The two pastors were forced by events to see themselves standing outside Protestantism, unable longer to belong to any group or school.[8] If the methods of reading the Bible did not provide protection against such perversions of the Gospel, something must be seriously wrong with those methods. (A similar observation can be made regarding theological education in every decade since). Here lies a major root of Barth's alienation from his exegetical colleagues.

Standing thus "outside Protestantism", the two pastors focussed their attention on the Bible and on the needs of their parishioners. "I tried to find my way", Barth wrote, "between the problem of human life on the one hand and the content of the Bible on the other."[9] Exegesis-as-usual was replaced by "a cry for rescue", a cry which could be compared to the cry of shipwrecked men, who had lost everything and were floundering in the waves. When their cry was answered, the "joy of discovery" separated them even further from the academicians. The more vigorous their own conversations with the Bible, the more sterile seemed the patterns of interpretation which they had inherited. They had moved into a world which seemed altogether different from the world of their exegetical mentors. In a letter of Oct. 6, 1921, Thurneysen wrote: "What kind of an earthquake region is this into which we have stumbled quite unconsciously in the very moment that we decided we had to read the New Testament a little differently and more exactly than our teachers."[10]

The new situation might be symbolized in terms of the number of desks at which they prepared their weekly sermons. Before they entered the "earthquake region" they had used two desks: one where they examined the text as the object of historical research, trying first of all to reconstruct the ancient situation; the other where they read the Bible spiritually and devotionally, listening for a message from God for his people.[11] But as successive Saturdays went by, these pastors found the separation of the two desks intolerable. Work at one desk pushed the Bible farther and farther back, making its world very strange and very old. Meanwhile at the other desk volcanoes were erupting and thunders rolled. Because the very strange world insisted on invading the present as a new and a true world, the two desks could no longer remain separate. This was not simply a matter of feeding suppressed desires; at times Barth would have preferred the earlier arrangement: "I am in haste for the time being to close the New Testament at this point and to busy myself with passages in which the fire does not burn so disturbingly."[12]

Thus the letters disclose the emergence of those attitudes toward the Scriptures which alienated Barth from the exegetes. Further light on this emergence is provided by lectures delivered by Barth during the years when the Commentary was gestating.[13] In these lectures Barth made very clear his evaluation of contemporary historical methods as applied to the Bible. On the one hand, he affirmed his reliance upon "the established results" of those methods. He agreed with that axiom of historical study, first expressed by J.A. Ernesti in 1732, that the Bible must be studied like any other human document. "It can lay no *a priori* dogmatic claim to special attention."[14] On the other hand, he challenged the adequacy of that principle in a strategic sentence, which in effect cancels it. "Intelligent and fruitful discussion of the Bible begins when the judgment as to its historical and its psychological character has been made..." Nothing could be more conventional than that;

it tips the hat to the prevailing deities of the academy. But the sentence continues: "Fruitful discussion begins ...when the judgment as to its human...character has been made and put behind us."[15] Those added words are anything but conventional; they dethrone the gods of the seminar room. The historian was bound to ask: "Why should all such judgments be put behind us before fruitful discussion can begin?". To this protest Barth gives a double reply. 1: The battle with "stark orthodoxy has been put behind us". 2: This human document has a "special content" which requires special treatment.[16]

This special content consists of the presence in the Bible of God's world, the world of beginnings and endings, "the deepest, innermost, surest fact of life."[17] In dealing with this world, critical reason is incompetent. "The reason sees the small...but not the large. It sees the preliminary, but not the final, the derived but not the original, the complex but not the simple...what is human but not what is divine."[18] The usual historical method may be able to grasp the human problems and questions, but it cannot lay hold of "the righteousness of God". It is designed to explore a zone of reality where God is absent and inactive, not the zone where God dwells with men and acts to save them.[19]

As Barth pictured the situation, the exegete stands at a window inside a house, watching the passersby in the street. Suddenly those passersby stop, look up into the sky, shade their eyes as they follow something hidden by the roof from the watcher inside the house. What do these men in the street see? "Something which is above everything, which is absolutely beyond the range of my observation and the measure of my thought."[20] Barth was himself fascinated by this discovery, and his whole Commentary reflects his fascination. "What a new world it is...And how remote we still are, merely in the outer court of this new world."[21] To Barth none of the biblical authors was more aware of that world - closed to the controls of the historical method - than was Paul: "Paul -- what a man he must have been...The Reformers, even Luther, are far from the stature of Paul...and then, behind Paul: what realities those must have been that could set this man in motion in such a way."[22] The "special content" of this document forces the interpreter to face problems for which the historical method has left him unprepared. With what categories does he deal with the realities "behind Paul"? When we consider the enigmatic character of those realities, as well as the excitement of discovering them, it does not seem strange that Barth should rely upon negations: "Biblical religious history has the distinction of being in its essence, in its innermost structure, neither religion nor history -- not religion but reality, not history but truth."[23] The reason for reliance on paradox is perfectly clear: this history is not history, this religion is not religion. It is wrong to dub the realities either historical or unhistorical. The categories do not fit the reality: "Biblical history...is not really history at all, but seen from above is a series of free divine acts, and seen from below a series of fruitless attempts to undertake something in itself impossible."[24] Thus in his early lectures Barth posed the problems which lay at the heart of his Commentary and at the core of his debate with his exegetical colleagues. Incidentally it was these same lectures which first introduced me to Barth's thought and which forced me to recognize within the Bible a "history which is different from all other histories," a history which therefore escapes the sieve of contemporary historians.[25] It is one thing, of course, to recognize the presence of God in human events, and quite another thing to know how to describe it. "When God enters, history for the while ceases to be, and there is nothing more to ask, for something wholly different and new begins -- a history with its own distinct grounds, possibilities and hypotheses...We may not deny nor prevent our being led by Bible 'history' far out beyond what is elsewhere called history."[26] Barth is by no means consistent in describing this reality: he may call it on occasion the non-historical, the history that is not really history, "true history", or simply history in inverted brackets.

In analyzing such antitheses, we may observe that the base-line of concepts is provided by the term history. Because the meanings of this term are protean, the antithetical terms will have multiple connotations. Until one meaning is nailed down, its opposite will blow loose. Barth accentuated the contrast without carefully nailing down the foil of his thinking. We may assume that the term "history" normally refers to that zone of reality which is amenable to the operation and controls of the historical method as applied by the professional historians of the day. Because so much escapes the net of that method, "the word history implies limitation and corruption." (<u>Commentary</u>, p.85). At any rate, the zone of reality covered by that method remains very narrow and thin. Not so the zone of reality to which the term "biblical history" refers. This reality exerts an ultimate and absolute claim. As such, it has its own "distinct grounds, possibilities and hypotheses". The usual modes of research are not capable of dealing with this 'history'. In fact, so long as scholars limit their exegesis to the application of those modes, they distort the reality to which the Bible witnesses. The result is this: "The history of religion has become the history of the untrue in religion, so that the truth becomes its non-historicity." (<u>Commentary</u>, p.69.). As T.H.L. Parker concludes: "The whole concept of history associated with the historical method comes under assault."[27]

There is an informative contrast between Barth and Bultmann in these early days; it becomes clear in comparing Barth's lectures with Bultmann's programmatic essay "The New Testament and Mythology".[28] Both men stressed the strangeness of the Bible; both were primarily concerned with the zone of eschatological truth. Both mounted astute attacks on contemporary forms of orthodoxy and liberalism. Both were keenly aware of the limits of the historical method in dealing with the message of the New Testament. However Bultmann conducted no such assault upon conventional historical methodology, but rather used it in such a thorough way as to command the respect of his colleagues. He did nothing to threaten the privileges or property rights of objective scholarship. He found in Heideggerian existentialism a way of dealing with the "wider" zone of reality that did not require an attack upon the assumptions concerning the historical process which were basic to the historian's work. Bultmann has had legions of followers, exegetes who have accepted his reconstructions of early church history, quite apart from their endorsement of his "theology". But Barth has had very few partisans among the exegetes, who have generally responded to his assault on their views of history by building a solid wall of defence. They have felt that his theological assumptions invalidated his historical work. They have refused to accept him as an exegete, being delighted to uncover numerous bizarre examples of <u>eisegesis</u> in his <u>Commentary</u>. The root of this impasse, I suggest, may be found in the contrary conceptions of history and of the temporal process which are imbedded in the dominant historical method.

Turning our attention now to the Commentary we will focus on one small segment, the treatment of Romans 13: 8-14. We select this text even though at first sight it seems to have no bearing on the problem of time and history. The text simply presents the demand for the love of neighbor as a way of fulfilling the Law. What is unusual about that? It is not surprising that most commentators deal with the text in an innocuous and banal fashion. Paul, however, relates this demand to a peculiar time-sense: "for now is our salvation nearer than when we first believed". To Paul, love is the measure of whether a person is living in the day or in the night. Even with this qualification, the command remains for most readers a pious convention. But Barth's seismograph detects beneath the surface of the text a volcanic disturbance. In the work of love, interrupting the normal flow of events, the two worlds, the two histories, are conjoined. Because it betrays an absolutely strategic relation between man and God, love is an "extremely enigmatic conception." (p.492). The love of neighbor becomes a test of our knowledge of God, the only mode in which we may love God. What is done to the neighbor, in all its mystery and untraceability, discloses what God has also done. In each work of love, therefore, there is a decisive <u>theological</u> coefficient.

There is an equally decisive Christological coefficient through the fact that the movement of Christian love is a response to the command of Christ. The victory of Christ was a victory of his love; the believer's obedience links him to that victory. It "points to the victory which has occurred, does occur, and will occur in Christ" (p.498). This makes the action of love an "essentially revolutionary action", in which the day of the Lord dawns, "the end of the world of time and things and men -- which is the Beginning" (p.498).

There is also a <u>pneumatological</u> coefficient in every deed of Christian love, inasmuch as it is a gift of the Spirit. Only the power of the Spirit can turn what is a religious impossibility into the possibility of God, i.e., the fulfilling of the Law (pp.493,494). Love is "the existential standing-before-God of men, their being touched by His freedom, whereby their personalities are established" (p.493). So love becomes an event in that history which transcends the Law, religion and everything that is "capable of analysis and description" (p.494).

By discerning these trinitarian dimensions in the work of love, Barth also discerned its eschatological ramifications. Since in love the old is overthrown by the doing of the new, this action marks the very dissolution of the course of the world (p.492f). Both the neighbor and the lover are introduced into a strange new world. Although this event is no moment in time, it becomes a parable of the eternal moment (p.497). Love proclaims "what hour it is"; by making visible the invisible new age, it becomes an incomprehensible, miraculous event between the times. In fact, something happens to time itself. The lover realizes that "it is not time that goes and comes; man it is who has been and will be in God, who dies and lives" (p.497). The same lover will, of course, recognize distinctions between near times and far, for the action of love requires such distinctions. But the tensions to which love attends are not those which can be measured by years and centuries, but are those which emerge from the contact between the temporal and the eternal. Love is an awakening from sleep to see the dawning of the Lord's day. This day is not "one period of time succeeding another" but eternity itself (p.500). Love has its own way of measuring the nearness of salvation. When Paul speaks of salvation as being nearer than before (13:11), Barth argues that this "has as much or as little to do with the well-known 1900 years of the history of the church...as it had with those weeks or months during which the Epistle...lay in Phoebe's trunk" (p.499). In such comments, Barth consciously challenged conclusions which had been current coin among biblical scholars since Wrede, Weiss and Schweitzer. More significantly, he repudiated the concept of linear time which has been assumed in modern historiography and which has been all too naively read back into the New Testament authors. There is hardly a scholar who does not attribute to Paul the notion of an end of the world, to be located on an objective time-line. Barth attacks them all: "The End of which the New Testament speaks is no temporal event, no legendary 'destruction' of the world; it has nothing to do with any historical, or 'telluric', or cosmic catastrophe.

BARTH'S COMMENTARY ON THE ROMANS, 1922-1972

The End of which the New Testament speaks is really the End; so utterly the End that in the measuring of nearness or distance our 1900 years are not merely of little, but of no importance...Who shall persuade us to depress into a temporal reality what can be spoken of only in a parable?...What delays its coming is not the Parousia but our awakening" (p.500). That awakening, Barth adds, is a matter of daring to love God and neighbor, that knowledge of the times which is expressed by readiness to stand on the frontier between time and eternity (p.501).

Parenthetically, let me remark on the character of Barth's debt to Kierkegaard. Much has been made of Barth's reliance, in his <u>Commentary</u>, on Kierkegaard's "infinite qualitative distinction between time and eternity" (p.10). Later on, Barth realized the inadequacy of that distinction, and, as we shall see, replaced it with the category of eternal time. I find even more significant, however, Barth's agreement with Kierkegaard in using the works of love as the best clue to the character of New Testament eschatology. In this respect Barth did not change. A study of the nexus between love and time in the two authors would prove worthwhile.[29]

Barth's treatment of love in Romans 13 shows how far his objectives differed from those of other exegetes. For him nothing displaced the desire for knowledge of God. "Paul knows of God what most of us do not know; and his Epistles enable us to know what he knew." (p.11) Because such knowledge transcends the changes wrought by the centuries, Barth wanted "to rethink the whole material and to wrestle with it" until the walls that separate our time from Paul's "become transparent", and that means "until a distinction between yesterday and today becomes impossible" (p.7). Most exegetes had quite different objectives, and neither side was ready to yield. When they accused him of being an enemy of historical criticism, he accused them of not being critical enough to measure the words of Paul by the matters about which Paul speaks (p.68). He believed that scholars who did not put first what Paul put first were bound to do violence to the text. To him, the Scriptures released an awe in the presence of the eternal which relativized most of the issues which the exegetes considered important. They, in contrast, encouraged an awe in the presence of history which led them to downgrade the significance of the apostle's word from the Lord (p.9). Their obsession with matters of detail induced from Barth the jibe that "in times of spiritual poverty, historical analysis is a method we are bound to adopt" (p.147). Quite apart from the question of its truth, such a sword-thrust does not conciliate opponents.

Typical of an extreme reaction is that of John T. McNeill: "When the philosopher, the theologian and the social theorist leave the stage, it is the historiographer who takes over. Humanly speaking, the last judgment is inscribed on Clio's scroll."[30] Barth could not share in such an evaluation of historiography. "The course of history does not in itself constitute the judgment of history" (p.58). When men assign to historical time the right to preside at the final judgment, time "continually slips away into infinity and is therefore lost forever". Time becomes the "abyss of our non-being".[31] Barth's view of the temporal process was far more favorable than that, since the works of love can redeem time in ways far beyond the historian's knowing. This contrast between McNeill and Barth may serve to summarize the state of the debate in 1922.

During the half century since, the lines of conflict have changed very little. To test this conviction, let us turn to a section of the Church Dogmatics in which Barth dealt directly and fully with the problem of time, in dialogue with three outstanding exegetes. I have in mind the chapter "Man in His Time" in the second part of Volume III. I do not suggest that Barth intended any correlation between Dogmatics and Commentary; nevertheless a comparison of the two will serve to bring out certain variables and constants in Barth's thought.

Many variables are quite obvious. Barth now writes no longer as a pastor but as a professor of theology.[32] His rhetoric is less explosive and more disciplined; his logic is woven more tightly. He explores each issue more patiently and extensively, carefully articulating each conclusion. He places less reliance on vivid images and tantalizing paradoxes, and gives opposing viewpoints the courtesy of more extended rebuttal. Into his argument he draws from both Testaments a wide range of biblical evidence. He often gives more prominence to data from the Gospels than the Epistles, and when he wants to clinch his argument he often selects an apt text from the Apocalypse. (The role of Barth as theologian might more often be compared to that of John the Theologue). There are also important shifts in vocabulary and categories. He is, for example, less prone to speak of "the strange new world" as being unhistorical or nonhistorical. Nor does he accentuate the distinction between time and eternity, as if the two worlds were bounded by that distinction. He is more likely to let the biblical history itself suggest the appropriate temporal categories.

For all these changes, however, we are nonetheless impressed by the degree to which the structural convictions remain constant. As in the <u>Commentary</u> we find warnings against the forced harmonizing of biblical thought: "Dogmatics has neither the occasion nor the duty to become a technical cosmology or a Christian world view" (III/2,p.6). "There is no world outlook which can be described as biblical, or even as Old Testament or New Testament, or as prophetic or Pauline" (III/2,p.9). In fact, Barth continued to insist that faith has always been "radically disloyal" to any dominant view of the world (III/2,p.8). He did not find such disloyalty among the exegetes; they, in turn, accused him of attributing to the Bible his own harmonized world view.

He approached his analysis of time as an aspect of anthropology (e.g. "Man lives in his time" p.437); but, of course, since man is viewed as a creature of God, his time becomes an aspect of God's activity. "God himself once took time and thus treated it as something real. But ... there is no such thing as absolute time, no immutable law of time. ... There is no time in itself, rivaling God and imposing conditions on him. There is no god called Chronos. ... As all creation has its goal in what God purposes and will do and does within it for man, for us, so time as its historical form has its meaning in the particular time which God once took for the execution of his purpose. ... This is the hidden meaning of all time. ... Time in itself has no property, no laws, to preclude the control of all other times by this time" (III/2,p.456). We cannot, therefore, know what time it is without knowing the will of God. The various times must be understood theologically.

This conviction that all times are controlled and therefore must be understood in terms of "this time of <u>Deus praesens</u>" (p.456) Barth considers as a corollary of the revelation of God in Jesus Christ. This revelation distinguishes and yet unifies the two histories, the two times of Jesus, one before and one after his resurrection.

Barth believes that we must safeguard the reality of both and interpret the significance of all other times in terms of their relation to these two. To say that Jesus is the Lord of time is to say that "like all other men, the man Jesus is in his time. ... the time he needs like all other men to be able to live a human life. ... He not only lives with God, but for him..not only lives with men but for them. ... It is this content of his life which makes the barrier of his time on every side a gateway. ... His time becomes time for God and therefore for all men...The answer given by the life of Jesus to the questions of God and man makes his time the time which always was when men lived, which always is when they live and which always will be when they will live. It makes this life at once the centre and the beginning and end of all the times of all lifetimes of all men...makes him the contemporary of all men" (III/2,p.439f).

There is thus in Barth's view a concordance between Jesus' first history and the history of all other men; but there is also an even more significant concordance between Jesus' second history and other histories, since this second history, the Easter history, reveals and ratifies the first. In dealing with the resurrection, Barth insists that "we are here in the sphere of history and time no less than in the case of the words and acts and even the death of Jesus" (p.442). Easter time is the time of Jesus, "the time of the revelation of the mystery of the preceding time of the life and death of the man Jesus. The two times are inseparably linked" (p.455). Easter time is also the time of God, the time of "the appearance and presence of God", "the time of all times because what God does in it is the goal of all creation and therefore of all created time" (p.455). "His eternity is authentic temporality and therefore the source of all time" (p.437). To be sure God "has a different time from that of men", but in Christ he has disclosed his decision "to give man a share in this time of his, in his eternity" (p.451). In Christ's time, God became temporal, making it clear that "his own time (is) at the heart of all the times of the being created by him" (p.455).

In our study of the <u>Commentary</u> we noted how the commandment of love became Barth's clue to the eschatological situation, since the work of love marks the dawning of the kingdom in both its presentness and its futurity. When measured by the frequency of the word, the notion of love is not so prominent in this section of the Dogmatics, yet the reality is even more pervasive than in the Commentary. Without reference to grace, the discussion of "man in his time" becomes empty. It is God's grace that is embodied in his gift of his eternal time "to the men of all time". He willed to have time for men "in order to inaugurate and establish his covenant". Men can have no share in this authentic temporality, this eternal time, apart from the time of Jesus, who "represents the grace of God". The Easter history, which makes Jesus "absolutely present temporally" conveys on them all the marks of being in Christ, all the rights of heavenly citizenship (p.467). Because he now rules over their lives, they receive from him whatever gifts of the Spirit may be needed (p.468).

The mastery of the times has thus been demonstrated by God, whose grace relativizes and diversifies all measurements of time. Grace limits and bounds our time, but includes it within his eternal time (p.568). "Death is our frontier. But our God is the frontier even of our death" (p.611). Because God is "wholly and utterly for us", his nearness or distance are not to be measured chronologically but by the dynamics of grace. Thus Barth leaves no doubt that he is dealing at every point with the love of God for men, though he postpones to other sections a detailed treatment of the commandment of love and its bearing on Christian ethics (p.633). What seems most clear, when we compare this section of the Dogmatics with the Commentary, is the accent upon God's time, eternal time, the two times of Jesus, as a reality which both limits and fulfills all other times.

In this same section of the Dogmatics Barth summarizes the issues on which he differs from his New Testament colleagues. He makes it clear that in his judgment they have defaulted on their basic responsibilities: "The time does not yet seem to have arrived when the dogmatician can accept with a good conscience and confidence the findings of his colleagues in Old Testament and New Testament studies...So long as so many exegetes have not better learned or practiced their part in this common task; so long as so many still seem to pride themselves on being utterly unconcerned as to the dogmatic presuppositions and consequences of their notions, while unwittingly reading them into the picture, the dogmatician is forced to run the same risk as the non-expert and work out his own proof from Scripture" (III/2/ix). When Barth takes up specific faults of specific scholars, he stresses their defective attitudes toward the temporal. Their presuppositions are such as to prevent the Easter faith from altering in any decisive way their prior conceptions of time. They agree in recognizing the full temporality of the history of Jesus in his life-time (p. 440), but differ in interpreting the temporal dimension of that "further history" which began on the third day after his death (p. 441). Let us look at his comments on three scholars.

Barth takes issue with Kümmel for failing to mention the resurrection in his book dealing with Promise and Fulfilment, as if that event were not "the axiom which controlled all their thinking about this man in His time" (p. 443).

He launches a sharper attack upon his colleague at Basel, Oscar Cullmann, especially for his defence of the thesis that biblical authors attributed to a system of linear time an independence and an absoluteness which was unaffected by their experience of the resurrection. "Surely it was a particular memory of a particular time filled with a particular history, it was the constraint under which this laid on their thinking, which formed and initiated their particular conception of time" (p. 443). Cullmann's fixed idea of time as a geometrically rigid ascending line with a successive series of aeons made impossible any thought of contemporaneity "between the history of Jesus and the prophetic history of Israel". To counter such a rejection, Barth writes: "Just as the tradition and recollection of (Jesus) makes Him the contemporary of the Church, so in the time of Israel the premise and expectation of His coming makes Him the contemporary of Israel. In both cases, it is a spiritual contemporaneity, perceptible only through him and only in faith. Where there is no revelation on His part or faith on ours... the history of Israel will become a history in which He has not come. The line of time, with its obvious differentiation of distance and proximity, then acquires... an absolute significance" (p. 481f.).

It was, however, with Rudolf Bultmann that Barth carried on his longest and sharpest debate; in this debate most issues centered on basic attitudes toward time and history. Bultmann, followed by most exegetes, so defined history as to deny to the resurrection of Jesus the status of historical fact. He did not allow to that 'event' any power to alter prior conceptions of the temporal process. He agreed with Barth, of course, in affirming faith in the resurrection, but he located this event "not in time but beyond it". It did not enter the zone of history where it could be dealt with by the historian "as an event in time and space" (p. 444); it could only be confessed by the believer as conveying the meaning of the Cross. To Barth, this dogmatic presupposition regarding the nature of time and history forces exegesis into an "anthropological straitjacket", distorting the entire range of early Christian thinking. He poses three questions for his opponent: 1: "Is it true that an event alleged to have happened in time can be accepted as historical only if it can be proved to be a 'historical' fact in Bultmann's sense -- i.e., when it is open to verification by the methods and, above all, by the tacit assumptions, of modern historical scholarship?" 2: "Is it true that the assertion of the historicity of an event which by its very nature is inaccessible to 'historical' verification ... is merely a blind acceptance of a piece of mythology, an arbitrary act, a descent from faith to works?" 3: "Is it true that modern thought is 'shaped for good or ill by modern science' ... (and that) this modern view (is) so binding as to determine in advance and unconditionally our acceptance or rejection of the biblical message?" (pp. 446f.).

Having now summarized the debate thirty years after the Commentary, what may we say about the prospect of a resolution of the issues outstanding in 1972 between Barth and the exegetes? It seems to me that the chasm is no less wide in 1972 than it was in 1922. Various exegetes have taken various initiatives to move beyond Bultmann, but none of these initiatives has basically challenged the dominance of Bultmann's conception of time and history. None has proposed any significant modification in the assumptions and methods of historical scholarship. There are exceptions, of course; but none of these individual scholars has attracted any substantial following. Among American exegetes, B.S. Childs mentions only Otto Piper and myself;[33] among British scholars we might mention E. Hoskyns and J. Marsh. Quite typical is the silence about Barth in a recent series of essays on The Significance of the Message of the Resurrection for Faith in Jesus Christ.[34] Of the three New Testament scholars who deal with this theme, none of them so much as mentions Barth. Moreover, in the leading article W. Marxsen demands an absolute separation between the historical and the theological approaches to the resurrection. He insists that as a historian no scholar can make any judgment about the resurrection as a historical fact. "Historical perception (i.e., historical exegesis) can always only state that witnesses claimed to have encountered God in Jesus" (p.21).

This unanimity in rejecting Barth is all the more surprising when we consider developments in other sectors. I have in mind such matters as these: the widespread influence of Barth in other disciplines; the growing disaffection with scientific methodologies as providing acceptable models for historical reconstruction;[35] the application to theological language of the insights of contemporary linguistics; the recent discoveries concerning time-consciousness on the part of novelists, dramatists and literary critics.[36] Exegetes are not noted, however, for their knowledge of what is happening in other disciplines; they are more likely to seek the plaudits of contemporary secular historians, even though this may mean endorsing assumptions which are no longer applied by the ablest of them. The cumulative effects of these and other developments may in the future produce a change in the patterns of biblical exegesis, but the changes which are visible today seem strangely devoid of Barthian influence. Rare indeed is any reference to the potential contributions of the Commentary to an understanding of Paul (e.g., in his own Commentary on Romans, C.K. Barrett gratefully acknowledges a vast debt to Barth for Christian faith but this indebtedness does not often extend to Barrett's understanding of Romans). It is not often that one can find among New Testament scholars any reference to the massive exegetical fine-print of the Dogmatics. We do not, of course, expect an imitation of Barth's style or easy agreement with his conclusions, but we expect a renewed effort to cope with those realities which Barth has shown were the prime concern of biblical authors. That kind of effort is no more visible today than it was in German biblical scholarship during the First World War. Historiography is no more capable of dealing with "the strange new world" than it was before its discovery by Barth and Thurneysen.

I do not wish, however, to end on a note of despondency.

The continuing impasse between Barth and the exegetes is simply an urgent invitation to examine the reasons for it. I believe that one reason lies in the choice of the major categories for dealing with the various realities under review. Both sides have adopted such terms as time, history, world, beginning and end, as if those terms had a common content on which both sides could agree. These terms, however, have lost their precision and therefore their usefulness. When used in discussion, their meanings shift so secretly and so subtly that mutual understanding is prevented rather than enhanced. So when Barth speaks of Easter time or eternal time, the categories themselves become obstacles to comprehension. Yet none of these categories is genuinely biblical, and no biblical category is roughly equivalent to them. There is urgent need to locate within the Bible an alternative vocabulary which can deal with the same realities without entailing the same difficulties.

For instance, in dealing with the relation of time and eternity (a relation which lies outside the zone of reality which historical methodology was designed to cope with), we would be wise to recover and refurbish the ontological categories of heaven and earth which are so pervasive in the Bible. Bultmann has done exegesis a great disservice by trivializing the biblical heaven, as if it were solely a mark of an outmoded cosmology, whereas it is frequently used as an effective cosmological metaphor to serve ontological and hermeneutical functions. Barth was more alert to recognize and to specify those functions. He recognized that when a biblical author speaks of heaven he often is thinking of a "time which is beyond time, space which has no locality" (Commentary, p.92). Heaven is indubitably real as "the sphere from which God speaks and acts toward man" (Dogmatics III/2/16). Or, as he writes in a later volume, "to say God in the biblical sense ... is also to say heaven" (III/3/419). The term functions as a pointer to "the divine horizon of human life", "the sum of the created reality which is invisible, unknown and inaccessible to man" (III/2/11; also III/3/424), "the sum of that which is really invisible or invisibly real" (III/3/425). These assertions strike near the mark of biblical modes of thinking.[37]

Yet in spite of its viability Barth forgoes any further use of this category and prefers the controverted terms time, history, eternity. Moreover, he uses these latter terms in ways which are bound to increase both bafflement and resistance. He seems to relish such paradoxical phrases as this: "the non-historical factor which is the beginning and end of history" (<u>Commentary</u>, p. 146). This, too, has done a disservice to exegesis by turning attention away from the reality itself to the language of the commentator. Bultmann's concept of historical time has proved too limited to do justice to those realities which Barth discerned "behind Paul" (III/3/375); Barth's concept has been too complex, too mysterious, too inclusive, to clarify thought or convey conviction. The complexities and the mysteries might, I think, be better conveyed by a more discriminating reference to those events in heaven which precede, correspond to and follow related events on earth. "Easter time" is a category which can hardly be assimilated into historical methods; the New Testament message concerning the continued heavenly activities of the Enthroned Lord creates difficulties; but I believe that here the difficulties are less insuperable. To be sure, the New Testament agrees with Isaiah that God's people requires a prophet to serve as its eyes (29:10), to see and to tell what is happening in heaven. But, given this prophetic vision, heavenly realities <u>can</u> become the basis of earthly life. Both Barth and Bultmann have, I think, underestimated the viability of the term heaven and the continued necessity of the role of the prophet as a revealer of heavenly realities. Barth tacitly expects the historian to fulfill the prophet's vocation; Bultmann is sure that no historian <u>as a historian</u> should attempt it. Post-Bultmannian exegetes are currently obsessed with the creative power of language. If they could supplement their often profound insight into language events with an equally profound awareness of the ontological reality of heaven and an adequate recognition of the work of the prophetic interpreters of heavenly events, they might be able to do greater justice to Barth's concept of eternal time. What continues to play havoc with the lines of communication between Barth and his exegetical colleagues is the fact that the Scriptures, which convey the prophetic disclosure of heavenly realities to the churches, have become the exclusive jurisdiction of professional scholars, whose vocabularies and methodologies have been created by secular disciplines to serve quite alien functions. We cannot expect any major change in this respect until Christian scholars mount their own liberation movement.

Relevant in this connection is a bit of humorous verse which in 1926 Barth considered the best review of Der Roemerbrief:

> "God needs men, not creatures
> Full of noisy, catchy phrases,
> Dogs he asks for, who their noses
> Deeply thrust into -- Today,
> And there scent Eternity.
>
> Should it lie too deply buried,
> Then go on, and fiercely burrow,
> Excavate until -- Tomorrow." (Commentary, p.24)

Barth viewed himself as such a dog, a dog of the Lord, who deplored the reluctance of his exegetical colleagues to burrow more fiercely into the Scriptures where he scented Eternity. On their part, his colleagues have found it virtually impossible to accept this burrowing as an essential part of their vocation.

Let me close by telling one of my most vivid memories of Karl Barth. During the years 1951 - 1953 he worked as a member of an advisory commission producing a working paper to be used at the Second Assembly of the World Council of Churches. We were meeting in Switzerland in 1953, giving final shape to a document on the theme "Christ the Hope of the World". After tumultuous and often acerbated debate, we had approved a final draft of three substantive sections. On the last evening we became convinced that a fourth concluding section would be needed. However, we were too exhausted to discuss in detail what it should say; so in desperation we turned to our most illustrious member, asking him to produce by the following morning a draft which could serve as basis for discussion. With a twinkle in his tired eyes he consented. The next morning he presented us with a draft under the heading "The Sum of the Matter". This draft was so simple, so lucid, so comprehensive, so representative, so cogent, that with very few amendments the Commission adopted it - a very rare thing in the life of such commissions. Some of the sentences in that draft apply not only to that single document but to all Barth's writing as well:

> "It is a human witness to a thing that is itself divine. We are well aware of the poverty and obscurity of our

expression of it. ... Among the earthly hopes of which we have spoken we must also place this one - that it may be given to those who come after us, in saying again the self-same thing, to say it differently, more clearly and more truly. And beyond that we await the eternal light which will at last illumine the darkness that besets even the best thoughts and words of sinful men."[38]

NOTES

1 The Epistle to the Romans, London, Oxford University Press, 1933, p. VI, tr. E. Hoskyns
2 The Word of God and the Word of Man, Grand Rapids, Zondervan, 1935, p. 100, tr. D. Horton
3 cf. Childs, op. cit., ch. 1
4 T.H.L. Parker, Karl Barth, Grand Rapids, Eerdmans, p. 16
5 Smart, Revolutionary Theology in the Making, Richmond, John Knox Press, 1964, p. 34
6 The Word of God and the Word of Man, p. 22
7 The Humanity of God, Richmond, John Knox Press, 1960, p. 14
8 Parker, op. cit., p. 19
9 The Word of God and the Word of Man, p. 100
10 Smart, op. cit., p. 75
11 For an influential statement of the "two-desk" position, cf. K. Stendahl, Interpreter's Dictionary of the Bible, New York, Abingdon, 1962, vol. I, p.420f.
12 Smart, op. cit., p. 48
13 "The Righteousness of God", "The Strange New World in the Bible", "Biblical Questions, Insights and Vistas", published in The Word of God and the Word of Man.
14 The Word of God and the Word of Man, p. 60
15 Ibid., p. 60, Barth's italics.
16 Ibid., p. 60
17 Ibid., p. 9
18 Ibid., p. 9
19 Ibid., p. 26
20 Ibid., p. 62
21 Smart, op. cit., p. 32
22 Ibid., p. 43
23 The Word of God and the Word of Man, p. 66

24 Ibid., p. 72
25 Eyes of Faith, Philadelphia, Westminster, 1946, p. 5
26 The Word of God and the Word of Man, p. 37
27 Parker, op. cit., p. 33
28 cf. Kerygma and Myth, London, SPCK, 1953, pp. 1-44, tr. R. Fuller
29 cf. S. Kierkegaard, Works of Love, Princeton, 1946, pp. 201-213.
30 Religion in Life, vol. 22, 1953, p. 586
31 Church Dogmatics, III/2, p. 521
32 The Epistle to the Romans, p. 23
33 Op. cit., p. 42f
34 ed. by C.F.D. Moule, London, SCM, 1968
35 cf. T.S. Kuhn, The Structure of Scientific Revolutions, Chicago, 1962
36 e.g. G. Poulet, Studies in Human Time, New York, Harper, 1956; A.A. Mendilov, Time and the Novel, London, Neville, 1952
37 A rare instance of exegetical indebtedness to Barth may be found in the essay on ouranos by H. Traub in Kittel, Theological Dictionary of the New Testament, tr. by G.W. Bromiley, vol. V. Traub relies extensively on Barth's treatment of heaven (III/3, p.369-531) and insists, against Bultmann, that this term at no point in the New Testament loses its symbolic character (V, 514). Rather it serves as an essential "integrating focus for the present and future blessings of salvation in the new aeon" (V, 532)
38 Christ - the Hope of the World. Documents on the Main Theme. Geneva, World Council of Churches, 1954, p. 39

JOSEPH C. McLELLAND

Philosophy and Theology - A Family Affair
(Karl and Heinrich Barth)

Karl Barth once wrote an essay in honor of his brother Heinrich, entitled simply Philosophie und Theologie.[1] His thesis is typically bold and engaging: "The opposition between 'Philosophy' and 'Theology' is (to mythologize a little) an Abstraction. What they truly have in common is the encounter of determinate men of diverse interests, commitments and engagements: the opposition and the association of Philosopher and Theologian". After a development of this thesis, Barth the theologian says to Barth the philosopher: "And if they are not only fellow-creatures (Mitmenschen), but wishing more earnestly on both sides to be Christian, then despite this last mutual reservation, it may be possible for them to behave according to the intention of Psalm 133:1. The Father of the Jubilar - to whom this book and therefore also this essay is dedicated - and of myself, used to call to us on certain occasions in our younger days, with finger raised: 'See, how good and lovely it is when brothers live together in harmony!'"[2]

That thesis and that insight from Karl Barth's mature years (he was 74 and Heinrich was 70; the year was 1960) provide the orientation for this paper. I will not attempt the impossible dream of showing that Barth was "really" open to philosophy, that he operated with a consistent view of the relation between philosophy and theology, or that he appreciated the philosophical options which his own theology implied. In short, I find myself in constant disagreement with Barth's position on these issues, despite my sympathy with his essential teaching. Or perhaps it were better to say: because of my indebtedness to him, I am free to engage him in debate! For he would indeed appreciate the irony of a Barthian "philosopher of religion".

There are too many questions in this area even to touch upon in one paper. Many of them seem strangely neglected (so far as I know) in the already vast Barthian secondary literature. Here are some questions that appear important for my present essai. How far is the early Barth, including the "earliest" Barth at Neo-Kantian Marburg (along with his brother Heinrich), determinative for the

PHILOSOPHY AND THEOLOGY - A FAMILY AFFAIR

later, despite the apparently dramatic shifts from the first Romans to the second, and the first Dogmatics to the second? What was Heinrich's influence at the formative stage, in interpreting Plato and Kant, in showing the way to a philosophy of appearance and event, and in reinforcing certain epistemological approaches that dominate the Dogmatik's view of thought and language? Are the two brothers to be regarded as complementary, as Karl's tribute to Heinrich suggests? If so, is Heinrich perhaps the silent partner, the hidden philosophical agenda behind much of Karl's vaunted "non-philosophical" assumptions? Or is it a case of Heinrich's being bound to theological premises as Karl is to philosophical?

Such questions remind us of the scope of any enquiry into Barth: and since he has claimed to be offering "an alternative to the mixophilosophico-theologia"[3] of modern thought, it is especially difficult to charge him with concocting such a mixture, however small be the philosophical ingredients, or however subconscious the recipe. In order to make my point I shall present sections on the transcendentalist problématique, the transitional research leading to the book on Anselm, and the constant aim of purifying theology as a scientific project.

(1) PROBLEMATIQUE: THE TRANSCENDENTALIST STANCE

The story of what Barth would later call "my trapeze work" as a neophyte theologian shows us how he and Heinrich learned about history from their father Fritz and attended Marburg where Cohen and Natorp were developing their distinctive kind of neo-Kantianism; and how Karl as pastor and professor struggled with his gigantic homework (scriptures, fathers, doctors, the newspaper) until he astonished the theological world with his Römerbrief of 1918. This early period has been examined almost ad nauseam, yet it remains one of the clues to Barth's position. He himself once remarked in a letter to Thurneysen that he had reluctantly come to see Luther's superiority over Zwingli on the doctrine of the Supper, "specifically in the study of the earlier writings of Luther, where one can see it as it comes into being".[4] Similarly, I suggest that Barth's relationship to the Kantian problematics remains a decisive orientation throughout his career. Kant's question was, How are synthetic a priori judgments possible? His aim was to provide a rational foundation for science,

31

despite the radical scepticism of Hume. His answer was to articulate the "transcendental unity of apperception" and to lay bare, through his critical Triplizität, the inherent rationality of human judgment in the face of truth, goodness and beauty.

There is a popular image of the early Barth as one who began with a Platonic-Kantian stance (I Romans), moved through a Kierkegaardian phase (2 Romans) and issued in a third and final stage thanks to the discovery of Anselmic method: Henri Bouillard has summarized the thesis well, and even Barth himself seems to have accepted it.[5] My counter-thesis is that the Platonic-Kantian base provides a constant, a permanent element in Barth's thought. For one thing, it presented him with the well-established anti-metaphysical tradition of Germany. If Ritschl is the name associated with this view, it was Herrmann, whom Barth called "the teacher of my student years", whose critique of rational orthodoxy involved a strategic and direct attack on metaphysics, which he considered a mistaken attempt to solve the ethical question posed by Kant.[6] Kant had driven reason beyond the antinomies of its pure scientific form, to achieve contact with Truth through a kind of moral positivism. The problematics of the Kantian system are grasped identically by the early Barth and the early Brunner, as they took up the debate with philosophical realism and idealism.[7] Both insisted that one must begin with a critique of reason, a mapping of its limited powers, and then must proceed to describe the rationality of an autonomous area of special knowledge. It is this general agreement with Kantian method that lends weight to the similar charge of at least one friend (Bonhoeffer) and one foe (Van Til), who claim that Barth is Kantian. Facing an unknowable realm of being, transcendental method accepts the dialectical response of the subject as the dynamic of epistemology, Bonhoeffer saw Barth's radical contingency of Act and Word as rendering "unequivocal theological statements" impossible, so that his dialectical theology paralleled Kant's "critical reservation".[8] His later charge of "revelation positivism" seems a logical development of this thesis, which we shall examine below.

Meanwhile, the question is, did Barth remain in the transcendentalist stance, the philosophical theory that man knows his world through a subjective act of unifying appropriation, and therefore speaks of this knowledge

PHILOSOPHY AND THEOLOGY - A FAMILY AFFAIR

through a language of dialectic? Is his intellectual pilgrimage, like that of his brother, a way from Kant through Kierkegaard to a more critical idealism? For Heinrich begins with a Philosophy of Practical Reason, 1927, which shows evidence of dialogue with the new Existenzphilosophie. He also displays similar interests to Karl: freedom in Augustine's thought, philosophy of existence, and at last his major work on philosophy of appearance.9 Let us reserve judgment on these Kantian-sounding signs, while remarking the striking unity of the brothers in their respective disciplines.

Kierkegaard has been mentioned: one fears and trembles to do more, for here the battle is indeed joined. Barth himself has stated that S.K. is someone through whose school one must pass; and one must pass. In his own "egg-shell" period symbolized by 2 Römerbrief he was able to execute a "turn of 180 degrees" thanks to the Danish catalyst.10 Barth claimed to have remained "faithful to Kierkegaard's reveille" which continued to sound like "a strong accompaniment (Unterton) next to others". Yet he scored the negative mood of such training in Christianity, and especially the Heils-individualismus that could offer foundation for a philosophy of existence and even a theology of subjectivity.11 The "Dank und Reverenz" which he owed Kierkegaard is thus charged to a definite period, a transition, when he was just the thing, the pinch of spice, to introduce a critique of idealism. Now the difficulty lies here, in the image Barth holds of S.K. and the subsequent image of Barth to be implied. Kierkegaard is taken as a type of irrationalist, helpful as therapy (after all, he called himself "a laxative"), stressing the notorious diastasis, the break, the "infinite qualitative distinction" and All That; but not much good on the positive side, the side of subsequent rationality, the constructive theology to which Barth was heading.

Alistair McKinnon charges that this is the image of a "phantom" S.K., the result of misunderstanding the intention of his pseudonymous utterances. The "real" Kierkegaard emerges through recognizing the authorship and the moving figure behind it. To grapple with the Kierkegaardian tour de force, argues McKinnon, is to drop the charge of irrationality and focus on paradox, and to identify the very stages or process which characterizes Barth himself. Therefore he can state: "At least in respect of the present crucial question, the position of the early Barth is identical

PHILOSOPHY AND THEOLOGY - A FAMILY AFFAIR

with that of the phantom Kierkegaard. Similarly, the position of the mature Barth is identical with that of the real Kierkegaard".[12] This view is part of an _apologia_ for the authentic Kierkegaardian voice; but it suggests "something about Barth" along the way. It suggests that he, too, began with the negative print, the inauthentic speech of diastasis, of those Kantian antinomies which break the ground to receive the positivistic seed; and that he, too, shifted not only to the positive pole but to an alternative understanding of the "rationality" of faith, beyond the paradox. If this is so, Barth is not - in his mature period at least - properly described as dialectical, as moving within a polarity of negative and positive; but rather he is one who renounces this earlier and Kantian substructure for a new base. I think McKinnon is correct about Kierkegaard; I am still doubtful about Barth.

(2) TRANSITUS - ANALYTIC A POSTERIORI JUDGMENTS

The key to our thesis rests with those transitional years from 2 _Romans_ to 2 _Dogmatics_. Two texts seem crucial for our purpose: the Dortmund lectures of 1929 (_Schicksal und Idee in der Theologie_), and the book on Anselm of 1931. Let me propose a query: If Kant's philosophical question is, How are synthetic _a priori_ judgments possible? is Barth's theological question, How are analytic _a posteriori_ judgments possible? For it seems clear from his work on Anselmic method that he came to see how theology is able (i.e., how it is possible) to make analytic judgments concerning the God who is revealed "in some other way".

The Dortmund lectures suggest Barth's initial research, forced by many pressures upon him after the dramatic shift of 2 _Romans_. The implications of his break with Harnack were becoming clearer, as Martin Rumscheidt's work displays.[13] The concept of subjectivity, clarified by the Kierkegaard study, had to be thought through in dialogue with Schleiermacher - I think that the significance of Brunner's _Die Mystik und das Wort_ in this regard might prove considerable, especially for Barth's own later reflections on Religion in its mystical dimension: "mysticism is esoteric atheism"![14] It was at this point that Barth sought to clarify his relation to philosophy, or rather to certain philosophical issues of epistemology or

PHILOSOPHY AND THEOLOGY - A FAMILY AFFAIR

objectivity. T.F. Torrance is particularly helpful in examining this period. He thinks that "The really decisive transition in Barth's thinking took place about 1930"; that it had to do with "the prior understanding of man bound up with a general anthropology"; and that "Barth swept aside all remnants of the language of idealist philosophy, even of Kierkegaard and particularly of the existentialist misunderstanding of Kierkegaard".[15]

Philosophy has halted between two opinions: the objectivity of <u>Schicksal</u> and the subjectivity of <u>Idee</u>. The first concept involves the question of what is real (<u>Wirklichkeit</u>)[16] and the second of what is true (<u>Wahrheit</u>)[17]. Thus Realism and Idealism emerge as Barth's subject-matter. Here is the overlap of philosophy and theology, in this dilemma of object and thought, one horn of which represents heteronomy and the other, autonomy. For the reality of object suggests that God is "ontologically and noetically man's Destiny". An uncritical stress on the statement "God <u>is</u>" leads to an objectivity which posits a necessary relationship between beings and Being, a heteronomous relationship that binds us <u>velite nolite</u> to God as Fate. Such <u>analogia entis</u>, however, misses the "critical realism" (if we may term it) which the Gospel introduces by its announcement that the Word took flesh. For now a modality of presence is revealed - presents itself - in which the Other moves towards us as a <u>Thou</u>. Yes, the <u>Ich und Du</u> terminology is explicit here, and another motif begs examination, the significance of the "Patmos group" with their vocabulary of Logos, of I-Thou encounter, of the reverberating Word.[18] For Barth, the Gospel represents the unexpected, the surprising news that our race towards Necessity has been interrupted from "outside" - and in such a way that the very "inside" of our subjective apprehension of that Act is itself part of this new reality. The natural and the necessary, matched by our knowledge and our acceptance - the realist dynamics of all that world of philosophy are challenged by Barth's theological analysis. Revelation here presents a new possibility, a God known not in his static inevitability but in his motion toward man, <u>in seinem Kommen</u>. This last point distinguishes the living God from Nature - and from Demons!

Idealism replaces the choice of heteronomy with one of autonomy. Distrusting naive realism, it places confidence in the act of knowing, in spirit. The sinister connection between idealist philosophy and mysticism is noted, along

PHILOSOPHY AND THEOLOGY - A FAMILY AFFAIR

with the further implication that this very connection warns us against simplistic reductionism, as if types of philosophy lead to only one theology. That is, for Barth there are parallels between philosophy and theology rather than logical connections. Both realism and idealism guarantee authentic elements in the structure of human knowledge, so that theology must always learn their lessons. Realism warns us not to forget the <u>givenness</u> of the object; idealism reminds us that the object is given <u>to us</u>, to human minds. This is not, for Barth, so much a polarization (as it was for Kant's response to the realism of Hume and the idealism of Descartes, for example) as it is a mutual critique, each one engaging in constant criticism of the other. Therefore here, Barth seems to reject Kantianism in a fundamental way, to deny the synthesis of the German tradition on behalf of genuine dialectic. If realism raised the spectre of Demonism, idealism raises another across the way - Ideology. For in accepting the idealist warning, theology may be tempted (Barth mentions A. Ritschl explicitly) to develop its abstracted thinking, its subjective logos, <u>die Welt des Geistes</u>, into the way to God. Barth grants Schleiermacher the mastery in this point at least, that he knew that "God is to be sought above these inner-worldly oppositions".

Barth's epistemology is already clear. He sees the human mind involved in both "spontaneity and receptivity", an antithesis which theology cannot escape. The question, however, is whether theology will be content to accept <u>both</u> sides of its dialectic from God, against certain idealist definitions of the power of discursive reason. Barth insists that theology is "science", but not simply one of the "human sciences" (<u>Wissenschaft, Geisteswissenschaften</u>). For its "object" is not a <u>thing</u>, to which the entire antithetical structure of reason applies; its "object" moves towards this structure from above it, rendering this entire "tension" (<u>Spannung</u>) responsible to a new structure. The new, theological, structure was described by the Reformers as "passive". It represents, for Barth, an "other" knowledge, which he describes as ac-knowledgement (<u>An-Erkenntnis</u>).

In the third section of the Dortmund lectures,[19] Barth reflects on the philosophy-theology relationship. Both occupy the same field, operate by the same dialectical movement, grapple with actuality and truth. But philosophy tries to have the whole say, to develop a synthesis that

will "solve" the problem. Against such an anthropology
or even theosophy, theology opposes its witness to revelation.
There is a contradiction to be expected as the
Word of God confronts the structure of human knowledge,
but it will be a different <u>kind</u> of contradiction from
that of the epistemological antitheses described. The
vaunted "synthetic art of philosophy" (<u>die synthetische
Kunst der Philosophie</u>) will not "solve" it. Therefore
where we find a self-limited philosophy at work, one that
describes and interprets the "actuality and truth" of man's
knowledge without turning itself into something more,
there we may find theology at work as partner, in a peaceful
coexistence.

Here is Barth's dilemma - still the Kantian problematics
to be sure: he wishes "philosophy" to be defined as <u>ancilla
theologiae</u>, a critical and limited exercise in epistemology
whose synthetic art will remain tentative and penultimate.
Insofar as it does so, theology may use it cheerfully. But
how can Barth seriously ask this of philosophy? Only if
he already assumes (subconsciously?) that the philosopher
grants the theological claim and therefore <u>defines</u> philosophy
in terms of the theological answer. Only if he
accepts theology's estimate of a Word of God beyond the
human antithesis can he understand his task as restricted
and partial. And here lies the weakness of Barth's position.
He is saying that the only good philosopher is a
Christian philosopher. He is defining philosophy as analytic
rather than synthetic, capable of descriptive metaphysics
but not of any sort of normative or fundamental
ontology. Indeed, only a Christian - only a Christian of
the Reformed Church! - could pass as philosopher in
Barth's definition. We think of Pierre Thévenaz or Paul
Ricoeur, both of whom would accept such a role for philosophy,
I believe. But how is one to meet those philosophers
who continue their synthetic work "as if God does
not exist"? It is significant that Barth draws his
Dortmund lectures to a close by examining the role of
theology, and appealing to the doctrine of divine election
as the final criterion of the true ideas of God. I doubt
whether such eschatological verification is viable in the
apologetic realm of debate with philosophers. I grant
that there is considerable evidence that Barth himself
was able to gain a respectful hearing from philosophers,
humanists and scientists by his straightforward declaration
of intention in his dogmatic work. But philosophers

who claim the freedom to pursue their synthetic task into concepts of man, of his religion, and of the object of his religion, will protest against the Barthian definition of their limits. As responsible philosophers they will accept no prior limitation upon their analysis of actuality and truth, least of all in the name of some alien Word which is poised somewhere above human structures. Not that this is a new problem, or one peculiar to Barth. But the dilemma seems clear: either philosophy itself will lead to conversion (<u>ex opere operato</u>), or else the only philosophical errors are the result of sin.

Barth's book on Anselm underlines the dilemma. Through his masterful analysis of Anselm, especially of the threefold <u>ratio</u> and the consequent path (<u>Weg</u>) for theology to follow,[20] he uncovers the similarity and difference between philosophy and theology. Both are involved with "truth in the second or middle circle", that is interposed between Truth in the ultimate sense and the human appropriation of its given form. There is a splendid sensitivity to Anselm's intention - Barth is one of the very few commentators to acknowledge that this is theology in the form of prayer, and not a textbook for introductory philosophy classes. The <u>remoto Christo</u> is understood therefore as a strategic shift, a deliberate device to unpack the logic of the revealed truth. But the analysis does not and cannot gainsay the revelation, the interposition from the side of ultimate Truth. So Barth's "analytic <u>a posteriori</u>" as I have termed it, is clearly on display in this work. Revelation creates a situation in which theological analytic shows how the actual is possible (indeed, "necessary"), but is not itself analysing the "other" revelation, "of God in his world", or "on other grounds".[21]

Barth is quite right to underline Anselm's intention, namely that the "existence of God" refers to a unique and peculiar <u>kind</u>. As the sole existence that is both ultimate and the cause of all other existence, it is "the only existence which in the strict sense can be proved"; by analysis it is proved also to be <u>necessary</u>, since "only the finite can be conceived as non-existing".[22] For our purposes it is not Barth's significant contribution to the long debate on the Ontological Argument that is important, but his adoption of the Anselmic method as that which honors the distinctive <u>theo-logic</u> of revelation. In this sense, he seeks to answer the Kantian problematic

PHILOSOPHY AND THEOLOGY - A FAMILY AFFAIR

by positing a second transcendence, beyond the entire human polarities and antitheses; and by ascribing to this Transcendent a synthetic art of its own, which embraces both poles, thesis and antithesis, in its reconciling arms.

A third text from this transitional period supports this view - the lectures on the Holy Spirit given at Elberfeld in 1929, along with a companion lecture by Heinrich.[23] Polemical and sometimes pedantic, the lectures show the greatest insistence on the all-encompassing role of Holy Ghost - Creator, Reconciler, Redeemer. The key concept is that every aspect of our hearing of the Word of God is God's own work - the familiar Barthian stance is consistent and unrelenting: any hearing we might call our own would be "only the echo of our own voice, in unbounded solitariness".[24] This statement occurs in the context of a discussion of sanctification; it foreshadows the elaboration of that doctrine that will occur in the Dogmatics, where again the point is driven home - even our "participation" in Christ's proper holiness is his work.

What is really at issue here? Who is the enemy that Barth so carefully hems in on both sides? Why does he differ so markedly from Tillich, who can write expansively of man's participation and mean it in its classic sense of ontological sharing, so similar to the Byzantine meaning? Indeed, is this latter perhaps a key, that Barth is terribly Western, Augustinian and that is what saddles him with the Kantian problématique? That is, is he so committed to a theoretical man-as-sinner that he must surrender every human philosophical epistemology and ontology to the mark of Cain? We know that his good humour proves irrepressible, that he is much better than his theory, that he is at home with "natural" man. That is an irony that he perhaps appreciated, but was never able to articulate within his system.

Here is where the work of Heinrich Barth may assist us. Like Karl, he began in that Marburg kind of Neo-Kantianism which may be summed up somewhat like this: a synthesis of Plato and Kant; acceptance of a critical method in philosophy; a stress on praxis, or applied philosophy; the updating of Kant in light of new mathematics and physics; a conviction that philosophy must obey Kant's own method and spirit, reject speculation and follow "the fact of science". Cohen and Natorp found themselves battling a new psychologism, and wedded their idealistic epistemology to the process of science, particularly the emerging

relativity theories. In part because of the fatal fact/
value dichotomy of modern thought, they appealed to an
immanentist idea of God to function as guarantor of values
(focus imaginarius). One can appreciate Herrmann's similar emphasis on praxis rather than speculation, and reliance on a quasi-positivism of revelation; even Vaihinger's
Kantian als ob theory fits well into this general approach,
while Cassirer (Cohen's pupil) sought for creative sources
in the category of das Symbolische.

Heinrich Barth's own work links up with this, as attested by Karl in the Foreword to 2 Romans: "the better
understanding of the real orientation of the ideas of
Plato and Kant for which I am indebted to the writings of
my brother, Heinrich Barth". His philosophical position
moved towards Existenzphilosophie about the same time
that Karl heard Kierkegaard's reveille. Indeed, Gerhard
Huber's survey of his thought distinguishes three similar
phases to Karl's: the initial critical idealism reflecting
Marburg school orientation; the transitional encounter
with concepts of freedom and subjectivity issuing in a
form of Existenzphilosophie; and a mature reflection on
the concept of appearance (Erscheinung).[25] His writings
on Plato's Lebensphilosphie and Kant's subjective consciousness converged towards a dynamic transcendentalism,
a formal-transzendentalen Idee as Aktfolge, source of
uniting power. He draws together existence and knowledge
(Existieren bedeutet Erkennen), but knowledge in turn
means to follow appearances (Existieren bedeutet In-die-
Erscheinung-Treten).[26] The concept of appearance or
phenomenon moves to centre stage, as he develops a cluster
of themes, notably the appearance as event and therefore
in tension with Idea: "Philosophical knowledge sees itself
therefore as called on to see through appearances to the
idea (Eidos) that dwells within it, yet without surrender-
ing itself again".[27]

The Philosophie der Erscheinung is a Problemgeschichte,
spanning the centuries from Socrates to Hegel, and attend-
ing to Being and Appearance as ontische Gegenpole. The
first volume (1947) traces the story to the end of the
middle ages, when the primary problem was that of contingency, the form which the appearance-problem was taking.[28]
The second volume (1959) - dedicated to the memory of Paul
Natorp - hails philosophy of appearance as "the open
window of philosophical knowledge". Noting the shift from
the Renaissance "magical consciousness" to the new

PHILOSOPHY AND THEOLOGY - A FAMILY AFFAIR

"mathematical" outlook of modern science, Heinrich Barth applauds the demise of the Platonic Apriorismus. Critical of the Cartesian reduction of being to selfhood, he provides in fact a history of philosophy, culminating in Kant's philosophy of Aesthetics. As a good Neo-Kantian, and therefore unlike our Anglophone approach to Kant, he sees the cruciality of the third Critique, where the facultas imaginandi comes into its own: both productive and reproductive, mediating between sense and understanding.[29] His conclusion is that philosophy of appearance opens on to philosophy of Urgrund, as Plato and Kant understood: from contingency of existence to revelation of being.

Gerhard Huber's analysis of Heinrich Barth's philosophy includes a valuable section on knowledge through faith in relation to philosophy and theology.[30] He notes Barth's insistence that the range of philosophical reflection must include the Christian truth, which offers a specific content to the philosopher. At the same time, faith agrees only with a limited or self-critical philosophy; and this is what the Kantian transcendental philosophy claims to be. Its stress on "mere humanity" leaves room for a grounding in God. There is thus a superiority of the knowledge through faith (eindeutiger Vorrang der Glaubenserkenntnis), deriving from the sheer weight of the Word of God. Because of this dimensional difference, no logical category can subsume both, which remain incommensurable. Philosophical knowledge is at best an "analogy of knowledge of God".

Here would seem to be a philosophical position in large accord with Karl Barth's views. It is a limited and critical philosophy, taking the category of freedom most seriously, and reserving strict causality to the positive sciences. Human freedom is the inverse of transcendental freedom, which may be geared into a doctrine of divine grace.[31] Heinrich also appears to agree with Karl that theology is "scientific" in nature, a reflex action set in motion by a specific sort of appearance, demanding an appropriate logical enquiry. There is, further, a self-criticism of the philosopher who recognizes in the diastasis between being and appearance, idea and reality, an irrevocable structure from the human side. And yet ... a trouble remains. Why does Karl deal so gently with Heinrich - especially in contrast to his harsh treatment of Brunner? Here is no Nein!, nor even a direct critique

of Heinrich's quest for some <u>Urgrund</u> that may or may not
be the Good, or God, or Nothingness. Is it a question of
giving the benefit of the doubt, or is there some "family
matter" hidden here? I do not know.

(3) TELOS: "THE MOST BEAUTIFUL OF ALL SCIENCES"[32]

Kant's ultimate question was: how is a science of metaphysics possible? Barth's is: How is a science of <u>theology</u> possible? And his answer becomes clear during the transition just examined: <u>by analyzing the necessary reasons in actual revelation.</u> His false start in <u>1 Dogmatics</u> was to begin with man, with the possibility of revelation, and so to show "reverence to false gods". Now he will move from the necessary to the possible rather than from the possible to the real. "It is not a matter of things that must be said in advance, but of things that must be said first" (I/1,41).[33] His quarrel with even Reformed orthodoxy is that its dogmatics were "too closely bound up with a form not taken from the thing itself but from contemporary philosophies"; that is why dogmatics must learn not from orthodoxy but from "Biblical exegesis in the actual Reformers' school".[34]

What is Barth's paradigm case for this actuality of revelation? It is the incarnate Word, the historical appearance - not mere phenomenon (<u>Erscheinung</u>) but because of the special history surrounding and attesting it (<u>Heilsgeschichte</u>), an unavoidable event (<u>Ereignis</u>). This summary could be illustrated from innumerable sources - notably the early chapters of Gifford Lectures, and especially the first volume of the <u>K.D.</u>[35] Because God is a speaking Other, his self-revelation "has its reality and truth wholly and in every respect - i.e. ontically and noetically - within itself". (I/1,350). The biblical testimony therefore constitutes "a self-contained <u>novum</u>", with exegesis, as mentioned above, the way to begin theology. Barth is therefore committed to the most serious grappling with the questions of time, history, and worldliness. He acknowledges here the help received from Heinrich on these very issues;[36] but his massive and consistent reflection is his own. Regin Prenter, commenting on Bonhoeffer's charge of <u>Offenbarungspositivismus</u>, seeks to honor that criticism by showing Barth's "actualism, analogism and universalism".[37] I believe there is much weight to Prenter's analysis. Barth commits himself

PHILOSOPHY AND THEOLOGY - A FAMILY AFFAIR

to a theology of appearances, so to speak, according to which revelation occurs in specific acts, not logically connected in a series - what Prenter calls a "point by point" view of revelation (je und je). If one does attempt a connection, a serial view, Barth calls it Religion - even Paul's Nomos is translated so.

Prenter's other terms, analogism and universalism, refer to the "platonizing language which is also found in the whole of the Church Dogmatics, in which there is increasing reference to 'correspondence', analogy, likeness, image, etc." It is the supra-temporal nature of revelation, according to this critique, which shows Barth's transcendentalism, and therefore his choice of cognition over being. Gustav Wingren has for long levelled a similar charge against Barth, that he is preoccupied with epistemology, with a paradigm of Incarnation. Although I would support this criticism to a degree, I think Barth provides some excellent counter-arguments. For one thing, he seems quite consistent in calling his so-called analogism an "exegetical decision", taken "under the compulsion of the object" of faith (II/1,227). He points out that the error of "anthropomorphism" belongs not only to crude, bodily ideas of divinity, but also to "spiritual" ideas - a point that Bonhoeffer himself makes in Creation and Fall. Moreover, his view of revelation as demanding an appropriate order of reasoning - the "scientific" method - implies the necessity of beginning with epistemology. Revelation gives, as "the order intrinsic to the theme", not analysis of divine being and then its activity ad extra, but the reverse: the ordo cognoscendi first, followed by but still related to, the ordo essendi (II/1,348ff). The passage is worth quoting: "The logical rigour of the dialectic which occupies us must not conceal from us the fact that we are not concerned with any sort of dialectic but with the very special dialectic of the revelation and being of God, in the apprehension of which we are not left to chance or caprice but must adjust ourselves to the order intrinsic to the theme, or realised on it. It is important not to miss this order if we are not to miss the thing itself". Here is the Anselmic method indeed: the ultimate Truth imposes its own ratio which guarantees the mind's conformity to its object only by the painstaking and painful (a catharsis is inevitably involved) backtracking on the way which this Truth has taken toward us. Analogy remains

PHILOSOPHY AND THEOLOGY - A FAMILY AFFAIR

"the correspondence of the unlike" (III/1,196). The divine accommodation or condescension involves a gracious opening of the Incomparable to certain analogies which serve to mediate and to heal; but all are the result of and therefore to be judged by, the mediator and healer, Jesus Christ. "In the reality of this event (in der Wirklichkeit dieses Ereignisses) God proves that He is free to be our God" (I/2,1).

The final question, then, is Barth's paradigm case, as philosophers would call it today, or the archetypal Analogue, in classical terms. At this point I find Karl Barth a most persuasive and attractive thinker. He knows that he operates within a circle - even Tillich granted that "kerygmatic theology" lies behind philosophical theology and describes the path to be followed. And if he can show that he is a theologian because of the special object to whose presence he witnesses, and because of the special science to which it calls him, then he will have made a prima facie case for his cavalier treatment of philosophy. In short, he will have established the autonomy of theology by identifying "God" in terms of a paradigm case - a form of analogia analogans - namely, Jesus Christ.[38] "Revelation does not differ from the Person of Jesus Christ" (I/1,134); "Jesus is the Lord ... can only be affirmed in an analytic proposition, as the beginning of all thought about it" (I/1,465). The name in question is a proper name, but it represents also the divine freedom to name himself through the "worldliness" which it involves. Here is the heart of any philosophical critique of Barth, where he discusses language. For instance, in the sections in I/1 on this topic, Barth deals with language in an "adoptionist" manner, as it were - just as he will deal with "religion" in I/2 ("one religion is adopted and distinguished as the true one before all others", 339). The "worldliness" which characterizes all the media of revelation means that the church is a sociological entity, the Bible a document of history of religions, Rabbi Jesus a founder, while theology - listen! - "so surely as it avails itself of human speech, is also a philosophy or a conglomerate of all sorts of philosophy" (I/1,188).

Does not Karl Barth want to have it both ways? He wishes to be free from all taint of mere philosophy, and yet time after time acknowledges the impossibility of that kind of freedom. It were, he says, a "grotesque comedy" to accuse

PHILOSOPHY AND THEOLOGY - A FAMILY AFFAIR

others of this or that philosophy, for "It is no more true of anyone that he does not mingle the Gospel with some philosophy, than that here and now he is free from all sin except through faith" (I/2,728). This section (727ff) is a denial of every sacrificium intellectus; that is, it is grace itself, Incarnation itself, which implies a use of philosophy - otherwise sinful man would cease from his sin, his worldliness, his situation in time and space. Therefore, Barth concludes, everything depends on "the How of this use" (730). And he makes it clear that he wishes to leave the beginning of everything up to scripture, to exegesis, so that in that light one may judge philosophies, whether and when and how to use them - and even Barth himself suggests, "I cannot radically exclude even the possibility that in certain circumstances, and for the better interpretation of Scripture, I myself will decide to use some quite different hypothesis, and even have to become a more or less consistent 'convert' to a different philosophy" (731).

The trouble I have with Barth is that his crucial definitions of both philosophy and science are too Kantian - that is, relative to and conditioned by this particular philosophical option - to carry the absolutist freight which Barth insists on. Philosophy, for him, is only a limited and dialectical theory of knowledge; science is that in which "an object is involved and a sphere of activity".[39]

There are, however, alternative definitions for both disciplines. Philosophy may, for instance, be dialectical as in Hegel and Marx; it may also be logistical as in Carnap or Russell; or inquiry as in James and Dewey. Besides that threefold division, we should ponder process philosophy's use of a Whiteheadian metaphysics, Maritain's classical view of the "universal science of being", and Husserl's Cartesian attempt to make philosophy "a strict science". The aims of both Maritain and Husserl raise the very question Barth is asking, perhaps unduly influenced by Scholz's concept of mathesis universalis (or Leibniz, finally, with a scientia generalis): is not theology the definitive science?[40]

Barth's loaded definitions of philosophy and science, I maintain, pervert his otherwise attractive definition of theology as the most beautiful science of all. His "dogmatic science" depends on his Kantian epistemology

PHILOSOPHY AND THEOLOGY - A FAMILY AFFAIR

in which "views and concepts" (<u>Anschauungen und Begriffe</u>) form the structure of human knowing. This structure is given truth (<u>Wahrhaftigheit</u>) when it is "adopted and determined to participation in the truth of God by God Himself in grace".[41] He bases this adoption on the principle that "God is known only through God" (<u>Gott wird nur durch Gott erkannt</u>). But this principle - that religious truth is self-evident - is not exclusively Christian, and is as compatible with mysticism as with Christian orthodoxy. Barth must face the harder question: is the Kantian epistemology the <u>only</u> adoptable one? If so, is this because it is already baptized by Christian influences, i.e. a crypto-biblical form of thought? That would be a subtle form of theological imperialism, fraught with grave perils. Or if not, then must not Barth admit that other structures may prove adoptable, so that alternative dogmatics will follow? It rather looks as if the Kantian philosophy functions as natural theology for Barth; or to put it another way, his criteria for adoptability are the "synthetic a priori" of his system, the hidden presupposition of his definition of the theological enterprise.[42]

Barth's idea of <u>science</u> reflects another point in his circular reasoning. He consistently defines dogmatics as a science: "we find ourselves in basic opposition to Philosophy, but we are all the closer methodologically to the inductive sciences based on observation and inference".[43] In his dogmatic prolegomena, however, he includes a section on 'Dogmatics as a Science' (I/1.7) which protests against restricting science to natural science. It would seem that in general, Barth has in mind the German concept of <u>Wissenschaft</u> - any consistent, disciplined intellectual approach - rather than the narrower English concept of science. But also, and in particular, Barth found science in its more positive or natural or inductive variety more compatible with his definition of theology as a special case. T.F. Torrance's recent trilogy of writings on this topic is most helpful here, not only because he has read Barth's grand aim properly but also because he recognizes the shift in "science" itself.[44] For, although Torrance uses the word in the sense of a universal or "basic way of knowing" which "applies to every area of human life and thought",[45] he also appreciates the dramatic shift in recent scientific method, in which induction has given place to a renewed role for hypothetico-deductive models,

PHILOSOPHY AND THEOLOGY - A FAMILY AFFAIR

to what Michael Polanyi means by the "tacit dimension" of knowledge, involved in the acceptance of "the logic of discovery" (Karl Popper) as the new paradigm. But if this is the form in which "science" appears today, it looks much less adoptable as a complementary discipline which knows its own limits, than Barth's image implies. To speak of "dogmatic science" therefore is not to beg a question so much as to tie oneself to a historical curiosity.

CONCLUSIONS

I have held that first, Karl Barth (as well as Heinrich) operates within a Kantian problématique, in that the polarity of real and idea, the dialectical structure of human knowing, is accepted as the correct description; second, the transitional work on philosophy and theology issued in theological actualism, positing credal affirmations as data for analytic thought; third, the aim of showing the scientific nature of theology itself is part of a Kantian package, and depends on tendentious definitions of both philosophy and science (and theology).

A major conclusion of the above is that Barth's "dialogue" with philosophy is not just ambiguous but self-deceiving. Thus on the one hand, he can study philosophers with sympathy and insight - witness the beautiful portraits of the first part of the Prot. Theologie im 19. Jahrhundert, and the passages throughout Dogmatics III where he engages Schopenhauer, Leibniz, Fichte, Nietzsche, Heidegger, Sartre. On the other hand, he frustrates his dialogue by concluding - almost intoning - that their view, concerns, axioms and goals have nothing in common with those of theology. Even the "nothingness" of Heidegger and Sartre comes to this: "seeing they do not really see" (III/3,348). Their blindness seems to result from their refusing a theological beginning, for ultimately the Word of God operates everywhere: philosophy "can be set in motion and then have power to move" (I/2,735). Barth's own epistemology, anthropology, ontology - and meontology! - constitute a proper "seeing", on the other hand, because they are open to a biblical starting-point.

A criterion of openness may appear pure, but in fact it itself has a Kantian ring. It was Kant who ended the classical tradition of philosophy as a way of obtaining knowledge, substituting a critical philosophy which operates

PHILOSOPHY AND THEOLOGY - A FAMILY AFFAIR

up against the limiting concepts (freedom, immortality, God for instance) that are reached by other means.[46] Barth likewise employs the limiting concept (Grenzfall) not only in his ethics[47] but in his theological analytic itself. For "the knowledge which establishes Christian language and doctrine" (II/1,186) involves a circularity that is posited by a radical Transcendent, beyond all limits and therefore in principle the absolute Noumenon. As we have maintained, Barth is far from ignorant of his situation. His dialectic of being and act moves toward a kind of "positivism of history" we might say, rather than of "revelation" (although he answered Bonhoeffer: "a little revelation-positivism is a good thing"). Where he posits a "third dimension" he breaks the Kantian dialectic, he moves around the epistemological circle far enough to offer a better perspective. That would be a matter for further exploration.

Let the last word be more positive - and more cheerful. In that same tribute to Heinrich, Karl stresses the co-humanity (Mitmenschlichkeit) of philosopher and theologian. Because neither can be "pure", both must work at common or similar questions, characterized by humility, and by humor. Each must resist the temptation to trade places with the other, as crypto-theologian here and crypto-philosopher there. In particular, when theologian plays philosopher he surrenders his proper work of the science of God: a crypto-philosopher, he states, is a pseudo-theologian, contributing to a theological history which becomes "a history of catastrophe". Barth's own zeal for his beautiful science, his jealousy for the name of God, his single-minded devotion to analysis of his paradigm-case, have been salutary for us all. If we find cause to quarrel, however deeply, let it be with similar humility and humor, not unmindful that at this very moment a rejuvenated Karl Barth is smiling at us - if he can take "time" to turn away aside from listening to Mozart (in person!) "with the angels".

NOTES

1 in G. Huber, ed., Philosophie und Christliche Existenz: Festschrift für Heinrich Barth (Basel: Helbing and Lichtenhahn, 1960), pp. 93-106)

PHILOSOPHY AND THEOLOGY - A FAMILY AFFAIR

2   Ibid., 106
3   Foreword to Evangelical Theology: An Introduction (NY: Holt, Rinehart and Winston, 1963), p. xii
4   January 23, 1923; p.126 of Revolutionary Theology in the Making, ed. Jas. D. Smart (John Knox Press, 1964)
5   Henri Bouillard, Karl Barth, Vol. I, pp. 17ff (Aubier, 1957); cf. T.F. Torrance, Karl Barth: An Introduction to his Early Theology, 1910-1931 (SCM, 1962), Part Two; and Karl Barth's speech Dank und Reverenz (E.T. Martin Rumscheidt, 'A Thank You and a Bow: Kierkegaard's Reveille' in The Canadian Journal of Theology, XI/1 (1965)
6   The theologians treated in the second part of Die Prot. Theol. im 19 Jhdt. illustrate the anti-metaphysical tradition before Hermann, with which Karl Barth identified his work.
7   cf. Barth's Dortmund lectures, 1929, Schicksal und Idee in der Theologie (in Theologische Fragen und Antworten, E.V.Z. 1957); E. Brunner's Religions-philosophie evangelischer Theologie (E.T. The Philosophy of Religion, London 1937), esp. 59ff
8   Act and Being (London 1962 - Akt und Sein: Transzendentalphilosophie und Ontologie in der systematischen Theologie, 1931), 83f
9   Philosophie der Praktischen Vernunft, 1927; Die Freiheit der Entscheidung im Denken Augustins, 1935; Philosophie der Erscheinung, 1946-and 1959 (complete Bibliography in Huber, op. cit., 251ff)
10 cf. on this whole problem Egon Brinkschmidt, Sören Kierkegaard und Karl Barth (Neukirchener Verlag, 1970), esp. 67ff, 'Die Paradoxie'
11 'Dank und Reverenz', op. cit.
12 'Barth's Relation to Kierkegaard: Some Further Light', Canadian Journal of Theology (XIII/1,1967), p. 37
13 Revelation and Theology: An analysis of the Barth-Harnack Correspondence of 1923 (Cambridge U.P.,1972) esp. Part Two, Evaluation.
14 C.D. I/2, p. 322. Brunner's work (Tübingen, 1924) reduces Schleiermacher too much in the direction of the mystical, whereas Barth (e.g. Theology and Church, essay 'Schleiermacher', esp. 186ff) appreciates his commitment to the "cultural" pole. My point is that Barth had to wrestle with this polarity before he was able to develop the reflections in the C.D. I/2 (K.D., 1938). cf. also the essays in God, Grace and Gospel

about his transitional studies.
15 op. cit., pp. 133, 139
16 Schicksal und Idee, op. cit., section 1, pp. 62-72
17 Ibid., pp. 72-82
18 cf. H. Stahmer, Speak That I may See Thee (Macmillan, 1968)
19 pp. 82-92
20 Fides Quaerens Intellectum, Zürich 1931, I.4: Der Weg der Theologie (E.T., SCM, 1960)
21 op. cit., pp. 117,138f
22 Ibid., pp. 99, 116
23 At a "theologische Woche", Elberfeld, Heinrich lectured on October 8 and Karl on October 9, 1929. Heinrich's was 'Die Geistfrage im deutschen Idealismus'; Karl's, 'Zur Lehre vom Heiligen Geist'. The two addresses were published in a Beiheft of Zwischen den Zeiten (Beiheft 1, 1930). Karl's was translated by R. Birch Hoyle as The Holy Ghost and the Christian Life (London, 1938) which bibliographical references erroneously ascribe to both brothers.
24 Hoyle, op. cit., p. 59
25 Huber, op. cit., esp. 'Epochen', pp. 200-202
26 Ibid., 207
27 Philosophie der Erscheinung, Vol. I (Basel, 1947), p. 122; the context is a significant discussion of the Chórismos between Idee and Erscheinung in the Platonic tradition.
28 op. cit., esp. VI: Das Kontingente Sein
29 Vol. II, (Zweiter Teil: Neuzeit), pp. 433ff
30 loc. cit., pp. 242ff
31 cf. Ulrich Hedinger: Der Freiheitsbegriff in der K.D. Karl Barths (Zürich, 1962), pp. 172ff for the remarkable accord of the two brothers on this point.
32 How I Changed My Mind (John Knox Press, 1966) p. 62: speaking of his two theologian-sons, "The sun now constantly finds at least one of our family awake and at work in the service of the most beautiful of all sciences".
33 References in parentheses will be to volumes and pages of the Church Dogmatics in E.T.
34 Foreword to Heinrich Heppe's Reformed Dogmatics (E.T., London, 1950), p. vi.
35 The Knowledge of God and the Service of God (London, 1938), esp. II: The One God; Church Dogmatics I/1, 28ff on the starting point for dogmatics; 226ff on 'The

Word of God and Experience'; II/2, sect. 13, on Christ as 'Objective Reality' and 'Objective Possibility' (in that order) of revelation
36 C.D. I/2, pp. 45ff
37 'Dietrich Bonhoeffer and Karl Barth's Positivism of Revelation' transl. by Martin Rumscheidt, in World Come of Age, ed. R.G. Smith (London, 1967). cf. Martin Storch on this question, chapter 1 of his Exegesen und Meditationen zu Karl Barths K.D. (München, 1964)
38 One of my doctoral students helped clarify this point - David Lochhead, The Autonomy of Theology, unpublished McGill University Ph.D. thesis, 1966, chapter 4, 'The Identification of God'
39 Dogmatics in Outline, p. 9
40 cf. Torrance, Theological Science, 107ff, 'General and Special Sciences' and the final chapter, 'Theological Sciences among the Special Sciences'
41 C.D. II/1, section 27, 'The Limits of our Knowledge of God'
42 At the Colloquium, David Lochhead and Herbert Richardson wished me to press this charge, of Barth's alleged "synthetic apriori". I prefer to remain more cautious on this point, since Barth's reading of Anselm itself faces the issue, as well as his self-consciousness about prolegomena. But I agree that the logic of my criticism is to show that Barth is essentially Kantian in bringing to the theological enterprise a theory of knowledge which functions as the apriori, the categories, in his theology
43 C.D. III/2, p. 12. In this brief excursus Barth gives a clear definition of science: "Exact science dedicated to its object and its method, working positively and not dreaming and romancing, is in fact pure knowledge ...". Now this itself is a form of positivistic philosophy of science, especially suited to natural science. Where science pushes on, e.g. to claim that a physiological description of brain is a contribution to normative studies of mind, how would Barth's criteria operate?
44 T.F. Torrance, Theological Science; Space, Time and Incarnation; God and Rationality
45 God and Rationality, p. 91
46 cf. Barth's essay on Kant in Die Prot. Theol. im 19. Jhdt. It is strange that Barth wishes there had been someone with "insight, courage and humour" to remind

Kant that the "irony" of placing philosophy and theology side by side has implications for both subjects; for J.G. Hamann (who, with Kierkegaard, is ignored in this book) did this very thing to his friend Kant.

47 cf. John Yoder, <u>Karl Barth and the Problem of War</u> (Abingdon, 1970) for a critical evaluation of Barth's reliance on the <u>Grenzfall</u> as paradigm

PAUL L. LEHMANN

The Concreteness of Theology: Reflections on the
Conversation Between Barth and Bonhoeffer

There is an amusing story about the last earthly meeting
between Karl Barth and Paul Tillich. The story may be
entirely apocryphal. Nevertheless, it seems pertinent
to our present assignment, and hence, a guarded currency
may be accorded it. It seems that after a cordial and
mellow visit to Barth in the Bruderholzweg, Barth accompanied Tillich to the nearby Haltestelle of the
Basler Strassenbahn. As they walked along together,
Barth put his arm around Tillich's shoulder and remarked:
"Paulus, as I think about our conversation, it occurs to
me that perhaps the real difference between your theology
and mine could be explained with reference to the legend
inscribed above the portico of the Church of the Nativity
in Jerusalem. Hic verbum caro factum est! Now, Paulus",
Barth went on, "you see, I have to have my hic!"
 Whatever may be the case with respect to Paul Tillich,
this "hic!" is certainly at issue -- perhaps decisively
at issue - between Karl Barth and Dietrich Bonhoeffer.
More critically still, this "hic!" is decisively at issue
in the doing of theology today. Abrasive as that phrase
is, to ears and sense accustomed to the ennobling ca-
dences of the Queen's English, it does express the perceptive and subtle evangelical sensibility of the author
of the Fourth Gospel. "But he who does what is true",
says the third chapter, at verse 21, "comes to the light,
that it may be clearly seen that his deeds have been
wrought in God." Or, as the New English Bible puts it:
"the honest man comes to the light so that it may be
clearly seen that God is in all he does." The integrity,
indeed, the possibility of theology today hang upon that
"seeing clearly"; upon seeing in and with the clarity of
light, as against the shadowy vagueness or the obscurity
of darkness, -- seing -- not God -- but what God is doing
in the world; and so, who God is. According to the
Fourth Gospel, the who of God is clearly seen in the
doing of God who "so loved the world that he gave his
only Son, that whoever believes in him should not perish
but have eternal life." (3:16)[1] Barth's own way of
trying to take dogmatic account of this doing and seeing,

THE CONCRETENESS OF THEOLOGY:

and explicitly of this text is to say that "God is He who freely loves".[2] As if to underscore the "hic!" which he has to have, Barth underlines the Vulgate rendering of the outos gar with which 3:16 begins. Sic! enim, says the Vulgate. Barth's "hic!" is this "sic"![3]

In a different context, namely not the writing of Dogmatics but the struggle of a church in statu confessionis with the principalities and powers in the heavenly and earthly places of this world, Bonhoeffer makes the same point. Speaking of "rigoristic and idealistic" misinterpretations of the Bible, Bonhoeffer asked in 1942: "But how is it, then, with John 3:16? ... The genuine relation between congregation (Gemeinde) and world develops only in faith in the revelation of God in the world."[4] Four years earlier, the point had been made with reference to 3:21. "The Bible", Bonhoeffer declared, "knows nothing at all about the pathos and problematic of the question concerning 'our way'. Our way ... has no weight of its own, no problematic of its own, and in particular no tragedy (Tragik) of its own. It is simply 'doing the truth' (John 3:21), wherein the accent falls wholly on the side of the truth. ... Along this way, to let Jesus Christ find us, this is our way."[5]

Whether one identifies the "truth" in the doing of theology with reference to "the Bible", or to "the revelation of God in the world", or to the "Who-ness" of the "God who freely loves", or to the "deeds which have been wrought in God", -- the hic! seems somehow insistently to haunt us. Try as it will, theology seems unable to get the hic! and the sic! together without succumbing either to the flamboyancy of rhetoric or to the tedium of repetition. As Thomas Mendip in Mr. Christopher Fry's "The Lady is Not For Burning" stridently declaims: "O tedium, tedium, tedium ... Where in this small-talking world can I find a longitude with no platitude?"[6] Somehow since Bultmann and Wittgenstein, and Norbert Wiener and Marshall McLuhan, and especially since Paul Ricoeur and Ernst Bloch have cut a door into Huit Clos! and lighted some alternatives to existentialism, we have begun to learn to live with ambiguities and semantic subtleties, with symbolizations and even paradoxes. But what disquiets us to the point of embarrassment and accelerates the flight from church and parish, from theology and prayer is the tantalizingly elusive concreteness without which no hic! commands its sic!; and every sic! -- as in

THE CONCRETENESS OF THEOLOGY:

the whispering gallery of London's old St. Paul's --
echoes with intensifying faintness the echoless <u>hic!</u> to
which it once belonged.
  Perhaps the nadir of our declining sensibility of the
concreteness indispensable to the significance and integrity of theology arrived in the course of a discussion
in my own theological faculty in late May of the present
year. Engaged as we had been, during the months preceding, with a concentrated and determined re-ordering of
our theological, educational and institutional priorities
for the immediate and for the long-range future, it was
inevitable and understandable that the question of a new
design for the program of studies and involvements leading to the Master of Divinity degree should be high on
the agenda. Without waiting for the agenda to elicit a
<u>nihil obstat!</u>, an <u>ad hoc</u> group of faculty and students
undertook to explore "the perimeters and the parameters,
the feasibilities and the negotiabilities", as the current
idiom vocalizes where we are and where we want to go. At
year-end in May, the faculty at large was invited to share
in a conversation about these idiomatic projections. Some
of us responded; and we learned that the focus was to be
on the "American experience" for the basic reason that
this is where we all were, and where we all came in, when
the doing of theology was what we were to be about. At
one point in the conversation, a black colleague expressed
some reservations about this point of entry into theological inquiry and explained that the "American experience"
effectively excluded his people who for three hundred
years in the United States had been effectively excluded
from the "American experience". Why, he then went on to
ask, had the <u>ad hoc</u> group not considered the Bible? The
Bible, he went on to explain, was where his people were,
and where they all came in, when the doing of theology was
what they were to be about. A long silence followed;
after which, two colleagues very much at the center of the
re-ordering of our priorities, replied by saying that they
would like to begin with the Bible but for them the Bible
was simply too remote to be of formative significance for
their own theological work. "But how is it, then, with
John 3:16?" What about the "Who-ness" of the "God who
freely loves"? or about coming "to the light, that it may
be clearly seen that (one's) deeds have been wrought in
God"? Clearly, where I live and work, the <u>sic!</u> is on a
runaway course in search of an authenticating <u>hic!</u>, with

THE CONCRETENESS OF THEOLOGY:

expectations at once eager and hesitant, frenetic and wistful, political and pluralistic. And this search goes on with a sobering candor matched by a sobering disproportion between theological self-confidence and theological seriousness! It's all as though Karl Barth and Dietrich Bonhoeffer had never lived and worked and died at all! Or is it because, <u>precisely</u> because, of what they did and did not do that our theological existence today is devoid of persuasive and freeing concreteness and vulnerable to idolatrous and cultic concretenesses filling the vacuum in our theological discrimination? It is as if "the unclean spirit has gone out of" us, and finding no rest, returns to find the house "empty, swept, and put in order. Then he goes and brings with him seven other spirits more evil than himself, and they enter and dwell there; and the last state of that man shall be worse than the first." Matthew, then, adds what Luke omits: "So shall it be also with this evil generation."7

Let us, then, attempt to "make the best use of (our) time" allotted to us by this gladdening occasion, "despite all the difficulties of these days". (Ephesians 5:16. Phillips) In doing so, let us attend in turn; (1) to the question of concreteness in theology; (2) to the relations between Barth and Bonhoeffer, as they were affected by this question; and (3) to some indication of a way ahead as regards the concreteness of theology, setting out, as we must, from where we are.

(1) THE QUESTION OF CONCRETENESS IN THEOLOGY

Although Barth and Bonhoeffer may have failed us as regards the question of concreteness in theology; and howsoever one may interpret the point at issue between them in their own debate, it can scarcely be denied that the concreteness of theology was a major concern of their theological work. In this concern, Barth and Bonhoeffer are still very contemporary; and whatever alternatives may now emerge (and some are emerging) can scarcely be serious alternatives in disregard of Karl Barth and Dietrich Bonhoeffer. Unable to re-read the <u>Kirchliche Dogmatik</u> from beginning to end for this occasion, and also unable to apply a computorial count to its pages, I have had to content myself with a scanning of the same. The survey shows that in the <u>Prolegomena</u>, the words: <u>konkret</u>, <u>Konkretheit</u>, together with their Latin equivalents: <u>in concreto</u>,

THE CONCRETENESS OF THEOLOGY:

concretissimum, concretissime, occur with conspicuous frequency. One encounters these terms with somewhat less frequency but no less noticeably as far as III/4. Less frequently and less noticeably, the words occur throughout volume four. If, then, one takes into account, konkret, Konkretheit, in concreto, concretissimum, concretissime and their cognates, e.g. Gegenstaendlichkeit, Wirklichkeit, Aktualitaet, Besonderheit, and the very frequent "nicht in abstracto", it is not too much to say that the driving pre-occupation of the Kirchliche Dogmatik is with the question of concreteness in theology.[8] That this is the case, is obliquely attested by the Registerband of the Kirchliche Dogmatik, which contains no entry marked: Konkretheit or concretum. Otherwise, the omission would be regrettable in itself, and also as an oblique indication of a subliminal disregard, on the part of the editors of the Registerband, of a widening distance between the Kirchliche Dogmatik and that "something major in the wind that is 'hammering our lives and psyches into new and unfamiliar shapes'."[9] In the writings of Bonhoeffer, as is well known, the question of concreteness is the focal point of his Ethics, for which his two major earlier books, Sanctorum Communio (1930) and Akt und Sein (1931) prepare the way, and from which the Widerstand und Ergebung (1951) delineates a movement towards involvement in a genuine worldliness.[10]

Yet two recent assessments of our present theological situation explicitly assert that the passion for concreteness which marked the theological work of Barth and Bonhoeffer has been spent or misspent. It is not clear which; but the consequences are the same. An article in the April issue of Theology Today asserts "the powerlessness of the western intellectual tradition, as it is now appropriated by us, to integrate and make sense of people's experience, to mobilize us for the tasks we face. The prophetic-apostolic witness, as part of this tradition, shares in its powerlessness ... Barth's theology," the article continues, "conceived originally only as a prolegomenon, became a massive system, and the old categories of thought, which arose to interpret human experience in earlier times, were reinstated. ... This road is closed to us."[11] The intellectual shift in our present cultural situation, which the authors of the piece in Theology Today underline, has been companioned by a socio-political shift in our cultural situation stressed in the

THE CONCRETENESS OF THEOLOGY:

course of the published meditations on the Fourth Gospel by Professor Frederick Herzog of Duke University, which arrived as this essay was in preparation. It is not merely co-incidental that neither Karl Barth nor Dietrich Bonhoeffer appear in the Index to Herzog's book. "The debate on revelation in twentieth century Protestant Theology", Herzog observes, "has been confounded by the fact that revelation was understood as disclosure of something that is hidden not only in fact, but also in principle. As we have seen, however, God is not hidden in principle. ... It is man's sin that hides God. The presence and future of God always reach man. The real trouble is that man does not acknowledge it."[12] Herzog's call is for "a re-ordering of theological priorities"; and this in serious and unfailing recognition of the fact that "In this society one cannot be a decent human being (Ernst Bloch). In this church one cannot be a decent christian . ... Theology today must begin with the wretched of the earth, the marginales, the marginal figures of life who are still struggling for personhood and dignity."[13] To begin here means, for us in the United States, as Herzog sees it, that "it is in the dialectical tension between black and white theology and in their confrontation that today we must take up again the task to describe what theology is all about."[14] Like the authors of the article in Theology Today, Professor Herzog wants and seeks to "narrow the gap between man's experience of faith and man's experience in history".[15] But unlike the authors of the article, Herzog thinks that there is an opening in the road, an opening provided at least, by the Fourth Gospel's version of the prophetic-apostolic witness. "... In the Fourth Gospel", he says, "we can almost touch with our hands the first full-fledged theological wrestling with Jesus of Nazareth as liberator. The pristine movement of Christian thought becomes important for us, so that our theological thinking might become more primal too."[16]

Clearly, these assessments of our present theological situation are preoccupied, as were Barth and Bonhoeffer, with the question of concreteness in theology. It is, in our view, regrettable that they have found it necessary to set the work of Barth and Bonhoeffer aside, however momentarily. Yet the theological seriousness, with which this disregard has been accepted as necessary, calls for a reciprocal theological seriousness towards the concerns about

THE CONCRETENESS OF THEOLOGY:

concreteness, which inform these assessments. To set these concerns aside with insensitive disregard, would mean a failure to discern the sense in which Barth and Bonhoeffer have not been overtaken by events in their own wrestling with the question of concreteness in theology. If such discernment were to be granted us, we should then also be able in some measure to point the way toward serious alternatives in distinction from alternatives insufficiently attentive to what Barth and Bonhoeffer have committed to us.

What, then, is the question of concreteness in theology all about? Among the remarkable qualities of the recently published Random House unabridged Dictionary is the vividness, directness and conciseness with which it exposes the semantic core of its entries. Thus, concreteness is defined as "constituting an actual thing or instance; real, pertaining to or concerned with realities or actual instances rather than abstractions."[17] With regard to instances or realities, to names as a class, in distinction from the qualities pertaining to them, the class is said to be concrete, the quality is said to be abstract. The word, man, for example, is concrete; the word, human, is abstract. It may be that no more is going on here than the differentiation between nouns and adjectives. But even if we suppose this to be the case, the distance between some adjectives and their nouns is greater than in the case of others. A more conspicuous abstraction occurs. The adjective "human", for instance, is less abstract when applied to the noun man than is the adjective, intelligent. Witness the lively debate now going on between Jean Piaget and Jerome Brunner over the what and the how of learning; or the intriguingly esoteric debate over the relation between syntax and reality which seems increasingly to be dividing Noam Chomsky from his students, and the brightest ones at that![18] The pertinence of these syntactical and pedagogical disputes over actualities or realities, i.e., over concreteness, to the question of concreteness in theology is the companionship which they offer theology in the misery of responsible analysis and interpretation; in what the Roemerbrief calls: die Krisis der Erkenntnis" (under the rubric of "die Schuld der Kirche") and die Krisis des freien Lebensversuchs (under the rubric of "die grosse Stoerung"); in what Bonhoeffer's Ethik calls: Gestaltung and die Struktur des vertantwortlichen Lebens.[19] More importantly, however, this reminder of the rabies

THE CONCRETENESS OF THEOLOGY:

scholarum humanorum to which the semantics of concreteness point, should underline the possibility that God just could be in somewhat better case. The theological tradition, however one may verbalize it, has insisted, at least since Paul of Tarsus, that God is the center and sum of all actuality and possibility, i.e., the "class" who is the beginning and the end of all "classification"; sic! concreteness. God's omniscience embraces both his fore-knowledge and his fore-ordination, so that both as primus agens and as summum bonum, he is concretissimus supremus sive absolutus. This can, of course, be a very abstract way of thinking and speaking, even concretissime. But let those who hasten too quickly to judge it as a terminal case of hic-amnesia pause to consider the possible impoverishment of their own capacity to discern the difference between the sound of words and their referentiality; as well as their own loss of cultural memory. Nevertheless, where theology falters in its task is not at the point of the concreteness of its warrant but in a fluctuating openness and steadfastness towards the concretissimus (be he object?, subject?, revelatus?, absconditus?: in fact? or in principle?) who is Alpha and Omega and Immanuel: behind and before and in the midst.

Thus, our colleagues, who through the pages of Theology Today have rightly been pressing hard the question of concreteness in theology "from somewhere along the road", might find it possible to discern, precisely in their situation as homines viatores, that intersection of two worlds in Jesus Christ, from which the Roemerbrief sets out,[20] and in the light of which, the KD is not really a massive system designed to enthrone old categories but a conversation of the people of God in all times and places about the God who takes time to be with people on journey and so meets them on the road. Surely this conversation in other times and places must be allowed to call us into question in our time and place as readily as we are called to call that conversation into question from where we are on the road. Just so, it may be that it has been given to these colleagues, exactly along their road, to rejoice in their deliverance from "programmatic" and "speculative" abstractions; and in their calling, to risk "the bold endeavor to speak about the way in which the form of Jesus Christ takes form in our world ... Concrete judgments and decisions will have to be ventured here. Decision and action can here no longer be delegated to the personal

THE CONCRETENESS OF THEOLOGY:

conscience of the individual. Here there are concrete commandments and instructions for which obedience is demanded."[21] Perhaps also, Professor Herzog, with like boldness, might find in his "political theology", which seeks to begin with "the wretched of the earth", neither an alternative to nor a displacement of "the great negative" and "the great positive possibility", with which der Roemerbrief concludes.[22] Perhaps in the very midst of the tension between those possibilities, a tertium quid may be discerned beyond God's hiddenness "in principle" or "in fact". The mystery of presence and pressure upon "the world of time and space and things, our world"[23], - under which and by which the marginales are being liberated, and to be liberated, for the human-ness which is their righteousness and their destiny, - transcends, in its sovereign majesty and purpose (its incomprehensibile and its incognito), the unrighteousness and suffering and sin in our world, and condescends in the miracle of Christmas, to be involved in that world, concretissime: vere deus, vere homo.[24] That happening -- then, and now -- is the center and occasion of a Magnificat -- again concretissime -- both in song and in the basic sense and structure of things. "The structure of responsible life", wrote Bonhoeffer, "is conditioned by two factors; life is bound to man and to God and a man's own life is free... Jesus Christ is man and is God in one. In him there takes place the original and essential encounter with man and with God. Henceforward man cannot be conceived and known otherwise than in the human form of Jesus Christ. In Him we see humanity as that which God has accepted, borne and loved, and as that which is reconciled with God. In Him we see God in the form of the poorest of our brothers. There is no 'man in himself,' just as there is no God 'in Himself'; both of these are empty abstractions. Man is the man who was accepted in the incarnation of Christ, who was loved, condemned and reconciled in Christ; and God is God become man. There is no relation to men without a relation to God and no relation to God without a relation to men, and it is only our relation to Jesus Christ which provides the basis for our relation to men and to God. Jesus Christ is our life, and so now, from the standpoint of Jesus Christ, we say that our fellow-man is our life and that God is our life."[25] Surely, it will have escaped no one that this is virtually a verbatim re-statement of the apostolic summation which Paul of Tarsus sent along to

THE CONCRETENESS OF THEOLOGY:

the congregation at Corinth: "With us, therefore, worldly standards have ceased to count in our estimate of any man; even if once they counted in our understanding of Christ, they do so now no longer. When anyone is united to Christ, there is a new world; the old order has gone, and a new order has already begun."[26] Thus, from a pauline, as well as from a johannine perspective, "concrete judgments and decisions will have to be ventured here". If, and in so far as, theology today must begin with the wretched of the earth, it is because "a new order has already begun". To begin here in theology is precisely to risk "the bold endeavor to speak about the way in which Jesus Christ takes form in our world". There are companions in this endeavor of whom Professor Herzog need not take account but who are not, on that account, less companions in the same theological venture concretely to make Jesus Christ concrete.

The distance between Barth and Bonhoeffer and their successors in the generation following is not marked by the presence or absence of a concern for the question of concreteness in theology. Where Jesus Christ is the concrete focus of the concreteness of theology, there need be no "middle wall of partition", (Eph. 2:14. AV). Instead, what Barth and Bonhoeffer have done, and what their successors are strongly urging must be done differently, is exactly what the concreteness of theology is all about. The profound disquiet over the abstractness of theology, which erupted in the Reformation, and then took a wrong turn from which the theologians of the nineteenth century had to rescue it, has come significantly into view with Barth and Bonhoeffer. It is the insistence by Barth and Bonhoeffer, upon the "actual instance" and "the realities pertaining to it" (Random House) that has brought the question of concreteness in theology to the present critical juncture. This juncture could be described in the following way: <u>Barth and Bonhoeffer are being asked by the oncoming theologians in our time to make sense of Jesus Christ in the midst of the culture and experience of a "world come of age"; whereas Barth and Bonhoeffer, in their turn, are asking the oncoming theologians in our time to make sense of the culture and experience of a "world come of age" with due regard to the concrete presence and pressure of Jesus Christ in our midst, "the same yesterday, today, and forever"</u> (Heb. 13:8). If Barth and Bonhoeffer seem at a critical distance to have been unable

THE CONCRETENESS OF THEOLOGY:

to bring their clearly resounding <u>hic!</u>, and a no less clearly resounding <u>sic!</u>, persuasively together, the task before their wistful and/or impatient critics is to match, with no less persuasiveness, their understandable passion for an unmistakeable <u>sic!</u>, with a corresponding passion for an irresistible, albeit dialectical, <u>hic!</u>

(2) THE RELATIONS BETWEEN BARTH AND BONHOEFFER

At this critical juncture, the relations between Barth and Bonhoeffer on the question of concreteness in theology may be looked at afresh. We need not review the story of these relations beyond the reminder of Eberhard Bethge's succinct account of their stages.[27] Bethge's account makes it plain that the principal concern which informed both their theological kinship and their theological disquiet towards one another, was the concern for the concreteness of revelation.[28]

Barth's first explicit reference to their kinship in this concern noted with approval Bonhoeffer's interpretation of the <u>imago dei</u> in <u>Creation and Fall</u>. There, the concreteness of the Creator's relation to his special creature is evident in the relation between male and female -- in the discreteness of each and in their reciprocity.[29] The special ethics takes account of Bonhoeffer's ethics as a genuine advance in exploring the concrete relations between the vertical <u>and</u> the horizontal factors in Christian faith and action. "Only insofar as the <u>vertical</u> intersects a <u>horizontal</u> can there be a genuine vertical", Barth wrote. "Due attention must be given to this horizontal, and on that account also to the specificity (<u>Stetigkeit</u>) and continuity of the divine command as well as of human action."[30] Bonhoeffer's notion of the mandates seemed to Barth to do just that and to illuminate, for example, Bonhoeffer's penetrating psychological and human interpretation of suicide, as well as to explain his participation in political assassination.[31] Barth's highest praise for Bonhoeffer appears in the penultimate volume of the <u>Kirchliche Dogmatik</u>, in the course of his own account of the <u>communio sanctorum</u>. Here, the <u>Nachfolge</u>, and even more, despite its sharp criticism of Barth, the <u>Sanctorum Communio</u> are impressively applauded, and with an open-ness which is not diminished by lingering reservations.[32] With reference to what Bonhoeffer called "<u>einfaeltiger Gehorsam</u>" (single-minded obedience), Barth

THE CONCRETENESS OF THEOLOGY:

declares: "That obedience is single-minded, in which a man simply does what is commanded: no more and no less, and nothing other than just that."[33] Barth agrees with Bonhoeffer that this is the concreteness of radical obedience.

From Bonhoeffer's side, the kinship with Barth started with the Roemerbrief. As Bonhoeffer began his teaching in Berlin in the winter semester of the year 1931/32, he addressed himself to the "History of systematic Theology in the 20th Century". The concluding section was devoted to the question "Where do we stand today?" "In the whole of the more recent literature", he remarked, "Barth has not been taken with sufficient seriousness. ... Perhaps in the Roemerbrief, the peril of proximity to neo-Kantian transcendentalism was not always clearly seen by Barth. But he begins with the concrete revelation; and where Natorp and Tillich say, 'No God' (Nicht-Gott), Barth must say, 'Jesus Christ'."[34] The significance of this remark is that it comes at the beginning of Bonhoeffer's own career as a theological teacher and within six months after the sharp attacks upon Barth in Akt und Sein, and a year and a half after searching questions put to Barth in Sanctorum Communio. Five years later, an exchange of letters, initiated by Bonhoeffer and replied to by Barth conveys in a lively way Bonhoeffer's concern for the actuality of doing theology with full candor towards the increasingly troublesome distance between theological students and the scriptural and dogmatic tradition. In turn, Barth replied with an openness and flexibility in the doing of theology which greatly impressed his younger colleague and critic. "The questions", wrote Bonhoeffer, "which young theologians seriously raise today are: how do I learn to pray? how do I learn to read the Bible? Either we can help them at these points or we cannot help them at all. ... Of course, these matters presuppose at the same time real and serious and unadulterated theological, exegetical and dogmatic work. I am clear about that. ... But I do not wish to by-pass these questions (ueberhoeren) for anything in the world..." To this, Barth replied: "Surely you will not expect from me anything but openness toward the substance of theology (Sache) and at the same time that I view it with concern. I am open because it is clear to me that in doctrine and in life always new questions must be asked, new attempts must be made... My concern arises from the experience of the past

THE CONCRETENESS OF THEOLOGY:

fifteen years which has found me under the steady fire of objections, and 'concerns', and amplifications ... the fundamental correctness of which I never could deny or wish to deny, but in the concrete explication of which ... I have become more critical because I have seen more clearly that ... such better solutions are like losing the sparrow in hand for the sake of the pigeon on the roof." What impressed Bonhoeffer was "how this man was able 'when necessary (noetigenfalls) to correct his notebooks."35

So Barth and Bonhoeffer seem to circle towards and then around each other out of their common and kindred concern for the question of concreteness in theology. For both, the concreteness of theology is its calling to make plain in and for the community of believers, which is the church, and in and for the world, the reality of God disclosed in his human-ness in Jesus Christ. Barth worries about Bonhoeffer's exploration and description of this concreteness, owing to what Barth regards as insufficient safeguards against the loss of the specificity of Jesus Christ. Bonhoeffer, on the other hand, worries about Barth's exploration and description of this concreteness, owing to what Bonhoeffer regards as insufficient safeguards against the loss of the human specifics to which the specificity of Jesus Christ is directed and with which it is involved. "Barth was never really comfortable with Bonhoeffer's directness"; writes Bethge, "he much preferred eschatological limits (Begrenztheit durch die Eschata)."36 According to Bethge, this may very well have been the point at issue, succinctly stated, about which Bonhoeffer wrote to Erwin Sutz, after his meeting with Barth in Berlin in April 1932. "Barth, however," he wrote, "does not agree with me on this point. This is now clear to me. Nevertheless, he raised the point again with me recently, and asked whether I still thought along this line. And he made it plain enough that for him, this point was still uncomfortable."37 Uncomfortable though it was, as late as 1936, in the letter to which we have already referred, Barth could say: "And now I see already that another wave is gathering, especially among the youth of the Confessing Church (Bekenntniskirche), in which then everything that has gone before will acquire new actuality, and it could even be that you are probably called and equipped to be spokesman and leader. If it should turn out this time to be no empty noise (blinder Laerm), I would hope not yet to

THE CONCRETENESS OF THEOLOGY:

be too old this time to learn what has to be learned, and necessarily to correct my notebooks, as I have already done in other respects. Meanwhile, however, you must understand if I simply wait."[38]

In this context, the increasing tension between Barth and Bonhoeffer over the question of concreteness must be understood. There is, we suggest, a link between the issue sharply raised in <u>Akt und Sein</u> and the hasty remark from the cell at Tegel, which greatly irritated Barth, and which those whom slogans fascinate, prefer to remember rather than to understand. In <u>Akt und Sein</u>, the passionate Lutheran engaged the unyielding Calvinist over the <u>finitum capax sive incapax infiniti</u>. From Tegel came, on the 30 April 1944, the vigorous letter to Bethge, in the course of which Bonhoeffer declared with regard to the relations between religion and Christianity, for which he was himself on the way to the phrase "religionless Christianity", that "Barth, who alone had begun to think along these lines, after all did not think these ideas through or carry them out, but arrived instead at a <u>positivism of revelation</u>, which in the last analysis, remained after all, a restoration (<u>Restauration</u>)." A week later came a more passionate, not to say intemperate, outburst on the same matter. "Barth", said Bonhoeffer, "was the first theologian -- and this remains his great achievement -- to begin the criticism of religion. But then, in its place, he set up a positivistic doctrine of revelation according to which the mandate is: 'eat, bird, or die' (<u>friss, Vogel, oder stirb</u>). Whether the doctrine concerns the Virgin Birth or the Trinity, or whatever, each doctrine is an equal and necessary part of the whole, that must, then, be swallowed as a whole or not at all. This is not biblical."[39]

The crucial point at stake in the tension over the <u>finitum capax sive incapax infiniti</u> is this: if the majesty and freedom of God towards the creation are too consistently stressed, the reality of faith on the part of God's human creature tends to be too radically called into question. The consequence is that the concrete humanness of Jesus Christ as God's concrete way of being God for us is obscured. On the other hand, if the reality of faith, as the direct experience of God in his concrete humanness towards man is too consistently stressed, the freedom and majesty of God, in the radicality of their priority and initiative tend to be insufficiently attended to. In the

THE CONCRETENESS OF THEOLOGY:

latter instance, the mystery of God's concreteness in his <u>self-revelation</u> loses theological force. "... the desire to locate in the act of belief itself the reflection which discovers faith only in the reflected form of faith-wishfulness, that is the danger of Barth. Faith and 'faith-wishfulness' lie together in the same act. Every act of faith is 'wishful' in so far as it is a happening embedded in the psychic and there accessible to reflexion. But faith properly so-called lies in the act's intention towards Christ, which is founded in being in the communion of Christ. A faith which grows doubtful of itself because it considers itself unworthy is a faith which stands in temptation. ... All praying, all searching for God in his Word, all clinging to his promise ..., all hoping in sight of the Cross, all this for reflexion is 'religion', 'faith-wishfulness'; but in the communion of Christ, while it is still the work of man, it is God-given faith, faith willed by God, wherein by God's mercy he may really be found. If faith wished to question its own sufficiency it would already have lapsed from intentionality into temptation."[40] This very Lutheran account of what we have since learned to call the existential reality of faith is what Bonhoeffer meant by his insistence upon the <u>finitum capax infiniti</u>. When Barth insisted upon the <u>finitum incapax infiniti</u>, he was exploring primarily the knowledge of God -- in faith and through faith, to be sure -- but as a cognitive act. For him, the neglect of the <u>incapax</u> on this front was tantamount to a natural theology which compromised the majesty and freedom of God in his self-revelation in Jesus Christ. For Barth, the <u>incapax</u> protected the concreteness of <u>God</u> in his revelation, as it were, on the giving end of the stick. For Bonhoeffer, the <u>capax</u> protected the <u>concreteness</u> of the <u>revelation</u> of God, as it were, on the receiving end of the stick, that is, in the reality of faith. For both, the major question of theology was the question of concreteness.

The failure of Barth and Bonhoeffer to meet on this issue underlies their more intense misunderstanding on the matter of <u>revelational positivism</u>. The gap had widened because of Bonhoeffer's increasing pre-occupation with the bond between <u>concreteness</u> and <u>non-religiousness</u>. The question: how can one speak in a non-religious way about God? about Jesus Christ? breathes through every line of the intense letter to Bethge. Somehow the reality

THE CONCRETENESS OF THEOLOGY:

of the communion of saints had come to include for
Bonhoeffer both believers and unbelievers because God
was and could be experienced in his concreteness in humiliation rather than in majesty, in suffering rather than
in sovereignty, at the center rather than on the edges
of life. This was the Lutheran view of faith as a lively
trust in the miracle of Christmas and of Crucifixion transposed to the context of a world come of age. For
Bonhoeffer, it is the reality of faith, however real its
knowledge may be, which excludes every kind of positivism
in theology. It is not surprising that Bonhoeffer should
have missed this kind of <u>concreteness</u> in the <u>KD</u>, especially
in the <u>Prolegomena</u>. Barth's own specific attention to
these concerns did not emerge until III/2 (1949) and in
III/4 (1951) and IV/2 (1959), where also his positive appraisal of Bonhoeffer occurs. By then, it was too late
for further exchange on these matters. It remains surprising, however, that Bonhoeffer should have read and
heard in and through Barth's epistemological pre-occupations mainly and strongly their positivistic leanings and
implications. This is surprising, not least because of
Bonhoeffer's expressed satisfaction with Barth's Anselm
Book;[41] but most of all because of their common involvement in the struggle of the Confessing Church against the
idolatry and tyranny of National Socialism. Without the
Barmen Declaration, there would scarcely have been a protracted, life and death church struggle; and without the
<u>KD</u>, there would scarcely have been Barmen. The record
suggests that the <u>KD</u>, far from being or functioning as a
massive positivist imposition to be swallowed whole, and
all or nothing, was in fact a theological arsenal for political conflict and liberation which made possible <u>concretissime</u> a confrontation between God concretely revealed
in Jesus Christ and the concrete principalities and powers
of the time. This does not mean that Barth's account of
the knowledge of God was invulnerable to positivist interpretation, and certainly to positivist use. What it
means is that Bonhoeffer's own movement towards "the
worldly sector"[42] had become so urgent for him that he had
lost sight of the more accurate substance and power of the
<u>KD</u> which was and is that it is not an architectonic compendium of theological <u>loci</u> but a polyphonic description
of the prophetic-apostolic reality to which the <u>Roemerbrief</u>
so powerfully attests.[43] We shall never know, of course,
whether, had Bonhoeffer lived, he and Barth would or could

THE CONCRETENESS OF THEOLOGY:

have corrected each other at this point. Nevertheless, we may perhaps say meanwhile, that the line from <u>finitum capax</u> to <u>religionless Christianity</u> in a world come of age is one indispensable side of the concreteness of theology. At the same time, it must also be said that the <u>finitum incapax</u> is the necessary companion piece if the concreteness of theology, whose concreteness is Jesus Christ, is to be nurtured and preserved from the alienation which could mean the loss of our theological existence today. To put it christologically, where after all, Barth and Bonhoeffer meet and go apart, the <u>vere deus</u>: <u>vere homo</u> must drive us toward and free us for "the man for others"; and contrariwise, the "man for others", apart from the <u>vere deus</u>: <u>vere homo</u>, sooner or later, loses his christological referentiality and becomes some other man.

(3) WO STEHEN WIR?

The debate between Karl Barth and Dietrich Bonhoeffer over the question of concreteness in theology identifies our theological place today. We need not repeat their language but we cannot elude their concern: its focus on the concreteness of Jesus Christ, and the boundaries dialectically drawn by the <u>finitum capax</u> and <u>the finitum incapax</u>; by the <u>vere deus: vere homo</u> and the 'man for others'. There are stirrings beneath the alienation and the secularity of our days which at the level both of culture and of politics suggest that where Barth and Bonhoeffer stopped, we are called to start. The New York Times of Wednesday, 25 October 1972, brought a review of a newly published book by Lionel Trilling called, <u>Sincerity and Authenticity</u>.[44] The thesis is that authenticity has displaced sincerity at the center of the culture and spirituality of our time, and with the dynamics and intensity of a religion. The credo is: "I'm authentic: therefore I am!" It is a piety for the mediocre whose aim is "to extricate themselves from the generality of the commonplace and stand forth in the authenticity of particular being". To this, Trilling's response is that "the falsities of an alienated social reality are rejected in favor of an upward psychopathic mobility to the point of divinity, each one a Christ...". <u>Finitum capax</u>! In the same week, Mr. Anthony Lewis reports that the only wife of a prisoner of war who refused to stand in applause of the recent assurances of the President of the United States of his unsleep-

69

THE CONCRETENESS OF THEOLOGY:

ing care, was shadowed by an undercover agent who was overheard to say into his "walkie-talkie": "she is now leaving the hall". <u>Finitum incapax</u>! "The Church", wrote Karl Barth, "...has always had to believe in the midst of the world what the world did not and also could not believe".[45] Bonhoeffer concluded his first course of lectures in Berlin with the remark: "our churchly messages are so powerless because they remain always in the middle between general principles and concrete situations. Luther could write the <u>de servo arbitrio</u> and the tract on the tribute money (<u>Zinsgroschen</u>) at the same time. Why can't we do that any more? Who will show us Luther? ...Where is the concrete principle for the demand for obedience?"[46] This open question is our question too. So also is our search for a faith for being human and for resistance in the struggle against the mounting arrogance and brutality of power. Perhaps these reflections upon Barth and Bonhoeffer over the question of concreteness in theology may quicken us to join them in their resolve and at our concrete place, where we are called to be. As Barth so humanly put it: "<u>Die Welt liegt im Argen</u>, aber <u>nicht war, wir wollen uns die Pfeife auf keinen Fall</u> <u>ausgehen lassen.</u>"[47] Perhaps the time is coming and now is (to borrow a familiar phrase) when Canada and her churches and theologians will be called to be to the United States as the United States was to Germany in the decade and a half from 1930 - 1945. <u>Refugium et virtus in statu</u> <u>confessionis libertate Evangeliique humanitas humanorum</u>.[48]

NOTES

1 The New English Bible says: "God loved the world so much that he gave his only Son, that everyone who has faith in him may not die but have eternal life."

2 Cf. Karl Barth, <u>Die kirchliche Dogmatik</u>, II/1, par.28. The paragraph is entitled: "Gottes Sein als der Liebende in der Freiheit", which I have ventured to translate as above, in some attempt to take account of the dynamics of God's reality (Being) in action (<u>esse</u> <u>in actu</u>).

3 Karl Barth, <u>Ibid</u>., p. 309; Eng. p. 275. The Vulgate reads at John 3:16: <u>Sic enim Deus dilexit mundum, ut</u> <u>omnis qui credit in erum, non pereat, sed habeat vitam</u> <u>aeternam</u>. The Greek text reads:

THE CONCRETENESS OF THEOLOGY:

οὕτως γὰρ ἠγάπησεν ὁ θεὸς τὸν κόσμον, ὥστε τὸν υἱὸν τὸν μονογενῆ ἔδωκεν, ἵνα πᾶς ὁ πιστεύων εἰς αὐτὸν μὴ ἀπόληται ἀλλ' ἔχῃ ζωὴν αἰώνιον.
As for verse 21, the Greek text reads:
ὁ δὲ ποιῶν τὴν ἀλήθειαν ἔρχεται πρὸς τὸ φῶς, ἵνα φανερωθῇ αὐτοῦ τὰ ἔργα ὅτι ἐν θεῷ ἐστιν εἰργασμένα.
and the Vulgate says: <u>qui autem facit veritatem, venit ad lucem, ut manifestentur opera eius, quia in Deo sunt facta.</u>

4   Cf. Dietrich Bonhoeffer, <u>Gesammelte Schriften</u>, Bd.III, herausgegeben von Eberhard Bethge, Muenchen, Kaiser, 1960, p. 452. Translation mine. Owing to the elision, I have altered the text slightly, without, however, changing Bonhoeffer's meaning. The passage comes from an essay on "The Lutheran Confessional Writings", with special reference to Baptism. Bonhoeffer had been asked by the Council of Brethren of the Confessing Church to deal with this question in view of a tract on Adult Baptism, published by a Silesian Pastor, Arnold Hitzer.
5   Dietrich Bonhoeffer, <u>Gesammelte Schriften</u>, Bd. II, herausgegeben von Eberhard Bethge, Muenchen, Kaiser, 1959, p. 324. Translation mine. The passage comes from an address given at a conference in Pomerania, to the illegal group known as "junge Brueder". The date was 26 October 1938. The subject was: "Our Way According to the Testimony of the Bible" (<u>Unser Weg nach dem Zeugnis der Schrift.</u>)
6   Christopher Fry, <u>The Lady's Not For Burning</u>, New York, Oxford University Press, 1950, p. 63.
7   Matthew 12:43-45; Luke 11:24-26. RSV
8   Compare the following random sampling from the original text of the <u>Kirliche Dogmatik</u>:
   I/1 -- pp. 141, 145, 155, 165, 262
   I/2 -- pp. 287, 403, 515, 667, 788, 897
   II/1 -- pp. 3, 13, 23, 53, 160, 296, 317
   II/2 -- pp. 2, 165, 226, 271
   III/1 -- pp. 2, 243
   III/2 -- pp. 174, 175, 270, 580, 639
   III/3 -- pp. 32, 216
   III/4 -- pp. 480, 558
   IV/1 -- pp. 96
   IV/2 -- pp. 104, 617
Such a random sampling suggests that a fruitful doctoral investigation of the KD would be the explicit and implicit

THE CONCRETENESS OF THEOLOGY:

   references to the question of concreteness in theology, and their constructive significance and limitations.
9 Karl Barth, Kirchliche Dogmatik, Registerband, herausgegeben von Helmut Krause, unter Mitarbeit von Wolfgang Erk und Marcel Pfaendler, Zuerich, EVZ Verlag, 1970. The vivid description of something happening between Barth and Bonhoeffer and ourselves has come to hand, as I write. It seems particularly appropriate in this connection, not only because of the imaginative identification of the intensity and depth of the search for concreteness in our time, but especially because the remark occurs in the course of a searching and serious "Essay on a Sermon" by a singularly sensitive and knowledgeable preacher and pastor of a christian congregation. Perhaps, we have come full circle; and where we all are, is where Der Roemerbrief started us all out a half century ago. "Barth's Der Roemerbrief After Fifty Years" -- sic! But see, Wallace M. Alston, Jr., On Discerning Good Faith from Bad Religion, in Interpretation, Volume XXVI, Number 4, October 1972, p. 454. Dr. Alston, who is Pastor of the First Presbyterian Church in Durham, North Carolina, quotes Alvin Toffler, Future Shock, New York, Bantam Books, 1970, p. 18.
10 As regards the question of concreteness in theology in the writings of Dietrich Bonhoeffer, attention may be called to the documentary footnote on the sources of the Barth-Bonhoeffer relationship in André Dumas, Une théologie de la Réalité: Dietrich Bonhoeffer, Genève, Labor et fides, 1968, pp. 21-22. The English translation is by Robert McAfee Brown, Dietrich Bonhoeffer-Theologian of Reality, New York, The Macmillan Co., 1971, p. 22. See also, Heinrich Ott, Wirklichkeit und Glaube, Band I, Göttingen, Vandenhoeck und Ruprecht, 1966, especially, chapters 4 and 6. The English translation is by Alex A. Morrison under the title: Reality and Faith, Philadelphia, Fortress Press, 1972. The question of concreteness in theology is, of course, what Sanctorum Communio and Akt und Sein are all about; and explicitly, the Ethics. The best treatment of the question, as regards Bonhoeffer's developing thought about it, is Eberhard Bethge, Dietrich Bonhoeffer, Muenchen, Kaiser, 1967, inter alia, pp. 228-28, 810, 960-61, 967. The English translation was published by William Collins Sons and Co., Ltd., London (1970) and by Harper and Row

THE CONCRETENESS OF THEOLOGY:

    in New York (1970). See especially pp. 131-42, 626, 759-60, 765.
11 Barbara Hall and Richard Shaull, From Somewhere Along the Road, Theology Today, Vol, XXIX, No. 1, April 1972, pp. 92, 96. Italics are the authors'. Bonhoeffer is curiously missing from these reflections. Hence one may be allowed to assume that in the view of Ms. Hall and Professor Shaull the perspective and direction of his theological thought also fail to open a road.
12 Frederick Herzog, Liberation Theology, New York, The Seabury Press, 1972, p. 257.
13 Frederick Herzog, Ibid., pp. 1-3.
14 Ibid., p. 2.
15 Barbara Hall and Richard Shaull, Op. cit., p. 97.
16 Frederick Herzog, Op. cit., pp. ix-x.
17 The Random House Dictionary, Unabridged, New York, Random House, 1967, p. 305.
18 A brief account of the controversy between Piaget and Brunner appeared on the first page of the second section of the New York Times of Friday, 20 October, 1972. On the syntactical controversy with Noam Chomsky, see the New York Review of Books, Volume xviii, no. 12, June 29, 1972, the article by John Searle: Chomsky's Revolution in Linguistics.
19 Cf. Karl Barth, Der Roemerbrief, 5te Auflage, Muenchen, Chr. Kaiser, 1929.
"Was sollen wir nun sagen? Sachlicherweise mussten wir, im Gegensatz zu den ueblichen schnellen und direkten Anklagen gegen die Kirche bisher einfach von ihrer Not reden. ... Die Erkennenden haben neben sich die Nichterkenndenden, die Kinder Gottes die Weltleute, die Heiligen die Unheiligen." (pp. 346-347; Eng., p. 362-63).
"Den Schluss der paulinischen 'Ermahnung' und damit der paulinischen Mitteilung ueberhaupt bildet eine Warnung, gerichtet an die Adresse aller derer, die sich nun vielleicht -- einverstanden und in ihren eigenen Gedanken bestaetigt fuehlen sollten. ... Wer wagt es die Freiheit nicht nur zu denken, sondern im Hinblick auf die Freiheit zu leben?" (p. 487; italics Barth's; Eng., p. 502-03).
Cf. also, Dietrich Bonhoeffer, Ethik, siebente Auflage, Zusammengestellt und herausgegeben von Eberhard Bethge, Muenchen, Chr. Kaiser, 1966.
"Nur selten mag eine Generation jeder theoretischen und programmatischen Ethik so uninteressiert gegenuebergest-

THE CONCRETENESS OF THEOLOGY:

anden haben wie die unsere. ... Das hat seinen Grund nicht etwa in einer ethischen Indifferenz unserer Zeit, sondern gerade umgekehrt in einer bisher in der abendlaendischen Geschichte nie dagewesenen Bedraengnis durch die Fuelle der Wirklichkeit konkreter ethischer Fragen." (p. 68; Eng., p. 64).
"Die Struktur des verantwortlichen Lebens ist durch ein doppeltes bestimmt: durch die Bindung des Lebens an Mensch und Gott und durch die Freiheit des eigenen Lebens. ... Ohne diese Bindung und ohne diese Freiheit gibt es keine Verantwortung ... Die <u>Bindung</u> traegt die Gestalt der <u>Stellvertretung</u> und der <u>Wirklichkeitsgemaessheit</u>, die <u>Freiheit</u> erweist sich in der <u>Selbstpruefung</u> des Lebens und Handelns und im <u>Wagnis</u> der konkreten Entscheidung." (p. 238; Eng., p. 224) Italics Bonhoeffer's.

20 Karl Barth, <u>Der Roemerbrief</u>, op. cit., pp. 3-7, Eng., pp. 27-32.
21 So Dietrich Bonhoeffer, <u>Ethics</u>, based on the sixth German edition, New York, The Macmillan Co., 1963, p. 88.
22 Karl Barth, <u>Op. cit</u>., pp. 459ff., 475ff., Eng., pp. 475ff., 492ff.
23 Karl Barth, <u>Ibid</u>., p. 5, Eng., p. 29.
24 See Karl Barth, <u>KD</u>, I/2, par. 15; II/1, par. 27.
25 Dietrich Bonhoeffer, <u>Ethics</u>, pp. 224, 221. The German text is pp. 238, 235. It goes without saying, or should go without saying that Bonhoeffer uses the words, <u>Mensch</u>, <u>Menschen</u>, in the generic sense.
26 2 Corinthians 5:16-17 NEB
27 Eberhard Bethge, <u>Dietrich Bonhoeffer</u>, p. 219; Eng., p. 134. Bethge notes the initial contacts, mainly literary, 1925-33. A third period involved the two in church-political activities in relation to the struggle with National Socialism. It was a time of theological distance. The fourth period echoed the first, as a period of new questions from Bonhoeffer's prison cell, and Barth's posthumous recognition of Bonhoeffer's early writings, 1944ff.
28 Eberhard Bethge, <u>op. cit</u>., pp. 220-228; 1054-56; Eng. pp. 135-42. The English translation omits the <u>Appendix</u>, to which pp. 1054-56 in the original refer. As regards specific exchanges between Barth and Bonhoeffer or systematic comments by each upon the other's writings, the most instructive are the following, from

THE CONCRETENESS OF THEOLOGY:

    the original texts:
      a) <u>Karl Barth on Dietrich Bonhoeffer</u>
         <u>KD</u>, III/1 - pp. 218-21, 272, 277;
            III/4 - pp. 2, 9, 14, 21-24; 460, 463, 513,
                687, 751;
            IV/1 - p. 74;
            IV/2 - pp. 571, 604, 612f., 626, 652, 677f.,
                725.
      b) <u>Dietrich Bonhoeffer on Karl Barth</u>
         <u>Sanctorum Communio</u>, pp. 94-5;
         <u>Akt u. Sein</u>, pp. 60-62, 67, 70-71, 74-79, 103-04,
              130-33;
         <u>Widerstand u. Ergebung</u>, Neuausgabe, 1970, pp.
              308-08, 311-13;
         <u>Gesammelte Schriften</u>, II, p. 41; III, pp. 76, 156.

29 <u>KD</u>, III/1 (1945), par. 41, 218-21; Eng., pp. 194-97. Bonhoeffer's <u>Schoepfung und Fall</u> was published 1933 (Muenchen, Kaiser); Eng., SCM, Macmillan, 1959.
30 <u>KD</u>, III/4 (1951), par. 52, p. 18; further, 20-24; Eng. pp. 17, 19-23. Italics Barth's; translation mine. Bonhoeffer's <u>Ethics</u> was first published in 1949; Eng., 1955 (SCM).
31 <u>KD</u>, III/4 (1951), par. 55, pp. 460ff.; Eng. pp. 404ff.; 512ff.; Eng., pp. 448ff.
32 <u>KD</u>, IV/2, par. 66, p. 604; par. 67, p. 725; Eng. p. 533; p. 641. This was 1955, ten years after Bonhoeffer's execution.
33 <u>KD</u>, <u>Ibid</u>., p. 612. Translation mine.
34 See Eberhard Bethge, <u>Op. cit</u>., p. 223. Eng. p. 137. Translation and italics mine. See further, Bethge, <u>Ibid</u>., pp. 1054ff. This Appendix material has been omitted in the English translation.
35 See Bonhoeffer, <u>GS</u>, II, pp. 286, 289. Bonhoeffer had written to Barth from Finkenwalde on 19 September 1936; Barth replied from Bergli, Kt. Zuerich, on 14 October 1936. Bethge records Bonhoeffer's reaction to Barth's letter in the biography, p. 223; Eng. p.137. Translation mine.
36 Eberhard Bethge, <u>Op. cit</u>., p. 225; Eng., p. 139. Translation mine.
37 Bethge, <u>Ibid</u>., p. 225; Eng., p. 140. Translation mine. The letter is dated, Berlin, 17 May 1932. See <u>GS</u>, I, p. 31.
38 See Bonhoeffer, <u>GS</u>, II, p. 289. Translation mine.
39 See Dietrich Bonhoeffer, <u>Widerstand und Ergebung</u>, 13th

edition, corrected and expanded, by Eberhard Bethge, Muenchen, Kaiser, 1966, pp. 179, 184; Eng., pp. 140, 144. Translation mine. The English translation renders the colloquialism: "like it; or lump it". The second letter was dated, 5 May 1944.

40 Dietrich Bonhoeffer, Act and Being, London, Collins, 1962, pp. 175-76. German pp. 149-50.

41 See Bonhoeffer's letter to Barth of 19 September 1936, already referred to. (GS, II, p. 285). In the letter to Sutz, Bonhoeffer wrote: "Barth's book on Anselm is a great joy to me... He exposes at last and in a basic way the countless crippling interpretations (Wissenschaftskrueppeln), and shows that he knows exactly and essentially how one can interpret and still remain sovereign." (GS, I, pp. 25-26) Translation mine. In the winter semester of 1932/33, Bonhoeffer lectured on recent literature in systematic theology and there discussed the Anselm book favorably. See, Bethge, Op. cit., p. 1081. This appendix has been omitted from the English edition of the biography. The puzzle is why Anselm did not mitigate the charge of positivism against Barth.

42 Dietrich Bonhoeffer, GS II, pp. 419-21; see also, Bethge, DB, p. 800; Eng. 626.

43 See Bonhoeffer's letter of 20 May 1944, in which the distinction between cantus firmus and polyphony is made, WE, 13th ed., p. 195. Eng., pp. 150-51.

44 Lionel Trilling, Sincerity and Authenticity, Cambridge, Harvard Press, 1972.

45 Karl Barth, KD III/3, par. 49, p. 234; Eng. p. 207.

46 Bethge, Op. cit., p. 1056. Translation mine.

47 Karl Barth in a letter to Dietrich Bonhoeffer, from Bonn, 4 February 1933. See GS II, p. 41. "The World is in dire straits, but we want - do we not? - under no circumstances to let our pipes go out." Translation mine.

48 The allusion is to Psalm 46:1: a refuge and strength in a confessional struggle for the freedom of the gospel and of the human-ness of humankind.

MARKUS BARTH

Current Discussion on the Political Character
of Karl Barth's Theology

I POLITICS IN THE LIFE AND WORK OF KARL BARTH

It is easy to enumerate moments in my father's life at
which he took an active political stance. Also there is
evidence of his interest and engagement in the last and
worst resort of politics, that is, in military matters.
Asked as a first grader in school to propose a sentence
for grammatical analysis, he suggested, "Wellington and
Blücher beat Napoleon at Waterloo." Soon after this legendary incident, the boy began to play enthusiastically with
tin-soldiers, and later he joined a youth cadet-corps.
Eventually, during World War II, he served as a volunteer
in the Swiss army's auxiliary troups. His assignment was
to guard bridges and public utility buildings against potential saboteurs. When he stayed in the United States
in 1962, he was not satisfied with visiting one after a-
nother of the Civil War battle fields and to astonish his
guides by his acquaintance with details of the battles;
he also fired twice a Confederate rifle, and his second
shot did not miss the mark - a coke bottle.
    Still, Karl Barth's engagements in political and social
issues were more permanent than his military exploits.
I will mention five instances:
    1. Between 1911 and 1921, the then minister in Safenwil,
Switzerland, gave the decisive impulses to the first organization of labor-unions in his parish. He gathered
male and female employees for educational sessions in
which he discussed the history of the labor movement, the
plight and right of labor in the Canton Aargau and elsewhere, and the goals, and short-comings of the Religious-
Social Movement, together with the tactics of the Social-
Democratic Party. Much time he spent in cantonal, fede-
ral and international meetings of the groups working for
social progress. He wrote articles for newspapers, gave
public addresses and intervened directly with some of the
'capitalists' in his environment. In about one out of
four sermons of that period he mentioned current political, social and economic issues - always in the frame of
the attempt to explain faithfully the Biblical texts he

had selected. It is, however, amazing that his sermons on e.g. Amos are not the most outspoken ones. In his fight against injustice and suffering he chastized the poor people's drinking and gambling habits as radically as the exploitation of labor by factory owners and managers. In 1915 he joined the Social-Democratic party. Also he pondered for a time whether or not to become a journalist or run for a political office. However, even before the Russian October Revolution damped his high hopes for the establishment of justice and freedom by political and revolutionary means, he decided against a flight from the pastorate. He chose to intensify the quest for the promise, the power, and the directive which came from a side totally other than politics, trade-unions or religious organizations. Beginning in 1916, Biblical exegesis became the instrument and criterion of this search.

2. When K. B., after the writing and rewriting of a Commentary on Romans, had become professor in Germany (in Göttingen, then Münster, then Bonn) he observed with horror a strong rightist movement among colleagues and students. On the theoretical level, a halo was provided for this tendency by e.g. Friedrich Gogarten's theology of authority. On the pragmatic side, the external and internal difficulties of the Weimar Republic seemed to cry out for the restoration of the good old imperial times. Marshall Hindenburg rather than the Social-Democratic Ebert was elected as Reichspräsident. The German churches and universities were harbors of conservative thought. For instance, Günther Dehn, a pastor in Berlin nominated for a professorship in Practical Theology at the University of Halle, was said to have suggested that a proper German war memorial ought to show a supersize sugar-beet rather than a heroic soldier or other symbol, for living from sugar-beets - this was what the war actually meant to the German people. Promptly a witch-hunt against this opponent of militaristic nationalism was started by chauvinistic students, and it found wide support or tacit condonation among professors, even among colleagure whom K. B. considered friends. Especially at the Open Forum held weekly in our home, but also in public declarations, K. B. sought to change the prevailing political attitude. His voice could not prevent the appointment of Adolf Hitler as Reichskanzler. During those years (between 1921 and 1933) wide circles accredited K. B.'s political stance to

his Swiss origin rather than to the substance of his theological work.

3. It is not necessary to elaborate on K. B.'s resistance against Hitler. Also his influence upon the formation and development of the Confessing Church movement is widely known. But three things I wish to mention: (a) The Barmen Declaration, while conceived as a 'theological' document for fighting (Nazi-influenced) heresy and disorder within the Protestant Churches, became de facto a backbone of political resistance, as exemplified by the Confessing Church's Prayer for Peace after the first Czecho-Slovakian crisis and by Dietrich Bonhoeffer's participation in an assassination plot. (b) At first it seemed that the Confessing Church had no other concern than the freedom of preaching and internal church organization. It appeared to have nothing to say in favor of the Jews, of ill-treated politicians and of suppressed minorities. And yet, from the beginning the Confessing Church was a political factor in Hitler's Germany. The Nazi regime was quicker to perceive this than were many devoted church members. (c) The reason for my father's ouster from his chair at Bonn University was not his blunt personal refusal to swear an oath of allegiance - though his qualified refusal was the occasion for his indictment by state authorities. He had insisted only upon the right and the power of the (Confessing) Church to declare that for all German citizens the validity of the required oath was limited by the contents of the First Commandment, "Thou shalt have no other gods before me." During these years the transition from K. B.'s Christian Dogmatics (1927) to his Church Dogmatics (1932-67) revealed a change of mind: What had looked like general reflections on the object and substance of faith, was replaced by instruction on how the church was to give responsible testimony in the political realm. The church as the people of God and as a social institution could not help being a challenge to tyrannical human powers. It was inevitable that this church should look like a provocation also to those persons and governments that were willing to make compromises with the world-view and new world order represented by Hitler. During World War II - especially in the periods when Rommel's armies made progress in North Africa - the Swiss Government was among those most unhappy with the political implications and expressions of K. B.'s thought. An opposite position

was taken only by the British Crown.

4. After World War II K. B. was, again, swimming Against the Stream. However, this time he fought revengeful attitudes toward Germany, the anti-communism which led to the Cold War, and reactionary political phenomena in - and outside Germany. He was engaged in this fight no less radically and eloquently than in his earlier battle against the religious and political goals of Hitler. Best known are his report on a trip to Hungary, his silence during the Budapest Revolt and its aftermaths, and his Open Letter to a Pastor in the German Democratic Republic. In those years, not only Dulles and Adenauer, but also theologians such as Emil Brunner and Reinhold Niebuhr denounced the position taken by him. As to his private judgement on the theoretical and practical merits of revolutionary communism, K. B. never wavered from the sharp criticisms uttered in the second edition of his Commentary on Romans, esp. in the interpretation of the 13th chapter of this epistle. However, together with the World Council of Churches Assembly at Amsterdam in 1948, he acknowledged the concern for social righteousness expressed by the Marxists despite their questionable accomplishments, and he refused to give religious sanctification to the superficial or hysteric condemnations of communism. The self-righteous attitude which, with or without benefit of clergy, dominated western churches, democracies, and dictatorships, was not deemed worthy of theological support.

5. The political character of K. B.'s theology was finally demonstrated by his attitude to prisoners. His preaching inside prison walls in a novel tone and language, was accompanied not only by his study for the whole penitentiary system, but also by extended and frequent private meetings with prisoners. When he offered a cigar to those he visited in their cells, it was not to announce the birth of a new baby, but to express his solidarity and hope. The freedom of God and the freedom of man, these main themes of his theological work, made it natural for him to work for Liberty to the Captives.

II QUESTIONS RAISED ABOUT THESE POLITICS

Violent opponents, admiring followers, and humble or cynical bystanders have been puzzled by the ever new turns of K. B.'s political involvement. Whoever - with pleasure or dismay - sees a red thread running through the several phases of his political engagement, faces questions such as the following:

1. Are the sketched attitudes and actions of K. B. nothing more than repeated, occasional escapades into ethical, political, social and other practical realms, that is, into spheres which in essence are strange and extraneous to the orthodox core of his theology as it is revealed in his book on Anselm and in the Christocentricity of his Church Dogmatics? An affirmative answer might include the charge of arbitrariness or ambivalence.

2. Or, it can be asked whether K. B.'s acts of participation in the political and social struggles of the various periods was as closely and loosely affiliated with his systematic, ontological, and exegetical exploits as is application to explication, or, practice to theory? Those who answer in the affirmative may express their admiration: K. B. did not remain in the safe enclosure of an ivory tower but ventured out into the ambiguity of life on the street. But they might also add the judgement, as does an early book of Charles West, that K. B., despite all his good theology, was a poor politician. In consequence, many would ascribe, as Jesus did in the case of the scribes and pharisees, according to Matthew 23:2 ff, authority only to K. B.'s teachings, not to the life style chosen and the actions accomplished by him.

3. Again, the question can be posed whether serious and competent political activity is characteristic of only "the young Barth"? If so, then perhaps the "young" man can be made to look as attractive as the "young Luther" appears to those bewildered by his later "dogmatical" utterances and stance. Some may go as far as to consider "Professor Barth" a traitor to "the Reverend Barth." Others, however, would conclude that the well-meant actions of the pastor in his theological egg-shells can and must be disregarded in favor of his more mature later works. Some may be inclined to consider the later resurgencies of the old, but primitive political spirit an equivalent to a relapse into the sins of youth.

4. The common elements of the mentioned three issues can be summed up in a fourth question: Is it necessary and feasible to discover a unity or uniformity that permeates not only K. B.'s complete theological work,

but also an essential harmony between his teaching, life, and character? Indeed, it is possible to demonstrate the unity of his doctrine and life in more than only one given period, or to delineate the progressive, but logical unfolding of a specific theological topic between 1908 and 1968, or to sketch with love and irony those personal idiosyncracies that survived or flourished in the face of ever new situations and challenges. In consequence, many a reader of K. B. makes his choice and selects the one Barth among the many he does not care for. However, doctrinal or biographical eclecticism may not be the wisest or most fruitful procedure. All too often, not only the critics of K. B. but also those apostrophized as "Barthians" live from such selectivity. They seem to be stuck with one single moment, method or element of K. B.'s work. But is K. B. perhaps taken seriously then only when the alternative "all or nothing" is faced and when even in slight details and obscure corners of this theology the unity of his witness is recognized?

III THE SETTING OF A REMARKABLE BOOK

A bold answer to these questions is given in Friedrich-Wilhelm Marquardt's book, Theologie und Sozialismus. Das Beispiel Karl Barth's (paperback, Munich: Kaiser, and Mainz: Grünewald, 1972). Several years ago, the author introduced himself to the academic public by his doctoral dissertation, Die Entdeckung des Judentums für die christliche Theologie. Israel im Denken Karl Barth's. The dissertation was written under the guidance of Helmut Gollwitzer, a professor at the Kirchliche Hochschule and the Freie Universität in West-Berlin. Because the latter was considered not merely a pink but rather a red theologian, he was not appointed as my father's successor at the University of Basel. Both Gollwitzer and Marquardt were and are deeply engaged in the struggle of the radical student movement in Berlin.

Some additional information about the Sitz im Leben of Theologie und Sozialismus will facilitate the understanding of its contents.

1. The latest book of Marquardt has grown out of lectures and seminars offered on the excited, explosive and volatile Berlin stage. While in his brochure, Studenten im Protest (1968), the author had tried to ex-

plain to bourgeois Christians the motivations of those students who could no longer pursue their studies as usual, he now intended to explain to the same students why K. B., who seemed to belong to the established ecclesiastical and bourgeois value system, is still relevant today. Marquardt is convinced that of all persons K. B. is the example, and that of all things his teaching is the stuff which the rebellious present student generation wants and needs. He expects that even if K. B. were oversold as a revolutionary socialist, the students would at least begin to read in K. B.'s works and learn from him how to think in dimensions neglected at present.

2. The editors of the German monthly Junge Kirche (33, 1972, 2-15) have done a disservice to the author of Theologie und Sozialismus by publishing his essay, "Socialismus bei Karl Barth", as late as three years after it was submitted to them. When Marquardt wrote this article he was not able to use more than the published political writings of the early K. B. Only later he volunteered and was chosen as the editor of the as yet unpublished collection of "Socialistic Speeches," which is stored in the K. B. Archive in Basel. Also, the huge majority of the complete Safenwil sermons were not yet in the process of being transcribed, not to speak of piles of other non-political materials dating from the same period. At any rate, despite the scarcity of resource material then available to him, Marquardt elaborated in the essay mentioned on four theses: (a) "Karl Barth was a socialist;" (b)"the Sitz im Leben of his theology is his socialistic activity;" (c)"in his turning to theology, he seeks to establish the organic connection between Bible and newspaper, the new world [of God's Kingdom] and the collapse of the bourgeois society;" (d)"the effect of this turn is the construction of a concept of God." The article in Junge Kirche appears to have been written with little care, and to be dictated by sensationalism. It has not only created great excitement, but also provoked sharp and well-deserved criticism. Still, Marquardt himself asks - and I should like to support this request - that he and his thesis be not judged on the basis of this article alone. For his (later) book Theologie und Sozialismus is the result of much more mature and careful, though no less passionate and exciting, research and reflection. It

may yet have been written and published too soon; Marquardt knew far too little of the total Safenwil activity of K. B., and rules laid down for the post-humous edition of K. B.'s literary bequest prevented him from quoting from the unpublished Safenwil materials.

3. Finally, a remark concerning the external, as it were mechanical, "setting" of the book: the cover of the paperback. Publishers and author had agreed that on the front cover a picture of K. B. should appear - in the company of images of Marx and Lenin. While the realization of this plan was prevented by the family of K. B., the previous announcement of the book at the Frankfurt Book-Show on a poster showing the three portraits harmoniously united, was beyond the family's veto-power.

IV THE CONTENTS OF MARQUARDT'S WORK

The substance of Marquardt's findings is dependent upon, and as astonishing as, the hermeneutics used in his study of and description of K. B.'s work. The author distinguishes between three senses of the writings: (a) the literal, (b) the intentional, (c) the existential, the latter being deduced from K. B.'s conduct. Most weight is placed upon the intentionality. Certainly, this hermeneutical method, especially the magnanimous discarding of the literal meaning and the context of many a quoted passage, is fraught with problems. Marquardt's interpretation of K. B. is so dynamic that often it looks divinatory, if not arbitrary. But because the eating rather than the preparation of the pudding proves its worth, Marquardt's work and its value are not only dependent upon its contestable methodology. I will try to sketch the substance of the book under five aspects:

1. According to Marquardt, K. B.'s theological work is motivated by two causes: (a) Left empty and hungry by the liberal theology he once had ardently studied, and facing its bankruptcy as demonstrated by the pro-World-War I declaration of the greatest among his German theological teachers, the Safenwil minister set out to find and formulate a <u>concept of God</u> that would be true to God and relevant to the world at the same time. (b) In seeing the plight of men, women and children in the factories of Safenwil and its environment, K. B.

studied and endorsed the <u>Marxist analysis</u> of the working class' predicament. Dissatisfied with both, the preacherly approach of Hermann Kutter and the political avenue of Leonhard Ragaz toward solving some of the vital problems, K. B. was looking for a new way to call for and establish social justice. In summary, the quest for the unknown God and the concern for social and economical righteousness were the two forces that made K. B. tick. According to Marquardt his question was: is there a supreme <u>logos</u> which controls and possibly brings into harmony the two seemingly contradictory <u>logoi</u> of a transcendent God and of a society immersed in material pursuits? In other words: Is there a way to show that and how the Bible is directly related to the newspaper, that the new world ushered in by God is connected with the need for total social change, and that the re-evaluation of all values includes the necessity of revolution? According to Marquardt K. B. learned to see that the two causes mutually condition and interpret one another. Certainly Marquardt's simplification of these most complex issues and relationships can be considered a sign of primitive, undialectical thinking. But his discovery of vital moving forces may also be interpreted as the mark of a genius.

2. Marquardt discovers in, or ascribes to , K. B. a special method of tackling the two issues before him. K. B. avoids the Scylla of hunting for an abstract theory or ontological system comprehending God or labor, and at the same time he bypasses the Charybdis of engaging in thoughtless, unreflected pastoral or socialistic practice alone. His book on Anselm has nothing to do with the imposition of a philosophical superstructure upon the <u>status quo</u> of societal order. And his activity as an organizer of labor is totally different from a blind capitulation to Marxist theory. Equally, neither the ministry of the Biblical preacher nor the organization of labor-unions was simply identified with the presence of God or the growth of his kingdom respectively. Instead, in successive steps the very being of God was described as a being in action, and God himself was conceived as "the reality that changes all things." <u>Esse sequitur operari</u> (being is the consequence of action) - thus Marquardt formulates K. B.'s emerging doctrine of God, in reversing a scholastic tenet. The active, effective, world-and society changing God displaces all other

concepts of God. In consequence, the theologian can no longer speak of an aseity of God (God's being himself, quite apart from his creation and relation to the creatures). It may be remembered that Whitehead and American process-theology argues similarly. Equally, according to Marquardt, K. B. refuses either to identify process, including revolutions, with God himself, or to separate total renewal of society from God - as if it could take place and succeed without him. Instead of cleverly combining or cruelly disjointing theory and practice, or, of separating explication and application, K. B. is engaged in an academically and politically motivated quest for true obedience to God's will in a communal life, in line with the order of God's kingdom. Unlike many philosophers, the theologian K. B., so argues Marquardt, does not intend to interpret God and/or the world, but to effect change. Since the alternative, "change the world,rather than interpret it," is also found in one of the Marxist Theses against Feuerbach, Marquardt speaks of a fundamental agreement between K. B. and Karl Marx. In other contexts the author also discovers a consensus between K. B. and Lenin, especially when the ultimate dispensibility of the state is discussed. Yet Marquardt adds a qualification to this consensus: K. B. stands far to the left of both Marx and Lenin! What makes the Reformed pastor so revolutionary that he must be, as Marquardt suggests, counted among the anarchists? Marquardt argues: While in his earliest years the Safenwil minister, true to his liberal teachers, attempted to follow or construct a way from the human yearning and potential to God, i.e. to ascend from man to God, he learned soon enough that the true way to know and obey God leads downward, even from God to man. K. B. discovered that God himself is the arch-revolutionary and his kingdom the source, driving power, and legitimization of revolution against the high and mighty on earth. For this reason K. B. had to fight Feuerbach who considered God a projection of wishful human thinking and to reject the bourgeois man-made religion which was concocted for nothing better than the sanctification of the status quo. K. B. proclaimed a God who is totaliter aliter, not in the wake of a lofty theory about a deity detached from and opposed to societal reality, but because he is the God who changes all things, including idealistic idols, Marxist ideology, social progress, and bourgeois fear of radical renewal. Augustine's discovery of the radical change effected by God in the individual soul was transferred by K. B. into the realm of the human community's material and social existence.

3. What, then, is the function of Jesus Christ in K. B.'s theology? Why does his Christology become more and more explicit and central? Marquardt's book contains intensive discussions of both, basic Christological dogmas such as the incarnation and subtle dogmatical niceties, among which Cyril of Alexandria's en- and a-hypostasy doctrine and the seventeenth century extra-Calvinisticum rank highly. However, it is Marquardt's bold thesis that K. B.'s theology is neither a derivate from his progressive penetration into the mystery of Jesus Christ, nor the result of the anxiety of the preacher (<u>Predigtnot</u>) who feels bound publicly to portray Jesus Christ, and nothing else but Christ. Rather the author affirms that the discovery of God's revolution, including its acme, the resurrection of the dead and the establishment of God's kingdom on earth, <u>precedes</u> the discovery of Jesus Christ's centrality and the (re-) formulation of Christological arguments. The two causes: theology and socialism, the two objects of research: the concept of God and a just order on earth, and the two resources: Bible and newspaper - all these pairs are fully present and active in K. B.'s thoughts long before he confirms and expresses them by Christological references, says Marquardt. The reality and indivisibility of "two natures" is fully recognized before the exclusive revelation in Christ, or even before incarnation and resurrection of Jesus Christ are made their eloquent and persuasive "symbols". Indeed in, e.g. the <u>Tambach conference</u>, the <u>Church Dogmatics</u> and the <u>Barmen Declaration</u> all emphasis is placed conspicuously upon Jesus Christ, the church and the Jews. However, this accentuation stems from the search of that which really matters: justice for the proletariat. Marquardt admits that the way toward Christology is a necessary feature of K. B.'s development. But while Christology <u>expresses</u> an ultimate concern, it yet is not essential to the substance of K. B.'s theology. Essential are and remain God and the proletariat alone. I will present two examples produced by Marquardt. (a) In his understanding of K. B.'s references to the extra-Calvinisticum, this doctrine means that the divine <u>logos</u> is present and works as ful-

ly outside Israel, Jesus of Nazareth, the Bible, the church, theology, as inside specific forms of his incarnation. Therefore the divine logos in person can be found in, e.g., the political revolutionary process. (b) The unity of the two natures in Jesus Christ means that not only the man Jesus but the totality of the human race and history exists only in essential and revelationary union with God and his will.

4. After the role of Christology has been defined in such terms, it is easy to state that despite all changes there is a basic unity in K. B.'s teaching and conduct. Admittedly there are differences or seeming contradictions between his early liberal and his later biblical theology; between the first and the second edition of his Commentary on Romans (ranging from wholesale endorsement of revolution to a revisionist stance, as Marquardt sees it); between the main foci or pastoral and professorial activities; and between the resistance against Hitler and the repudiation of anti-communism; between the voice raised in public concerning world-shaking matters and the hidden work for prison-inmates. But K. B.'s theology never pretended to form a solid and tightly-woven system. A fixed definition of a specific concept of God would have been considered by him as idolatrous as an unqualified endorsement of the Russian revolution or its opposite, the Brunner-Niebuhr-Dulles form of combatting communism. What kept K. B.'s theology together was neither a principle, nor definitions, nor a position but the way which he had to follow. In his thought and conduct K. B. did nothing else than follow the way of God toward man, even the divine inroad into the disorder of society. This means, according to Marquardt, that every phase of K. B.'s life and every page of his Dogmatics are equally political. If it is God's nature to effect total change then a theologian must in word and deed participate in changing the social conditions.

5. The most radical agent and carrier of God's revolution is the church. When K. B. did not quit the pastorate, when even as a professor he remained a preacher, when he called his main work Church Dogmatics, and when he contributed to the foundation and the course of the Confessing Church movement, he demonstrated that the strongest witness to God's revolution is borne neither by passionate individuals nor by the progress of world

POLITICAL CHARACTER OF KARL BARTH'S THEOLOGY

history alone, but rather by a very specific society, the church. Therefore, the ecclesiastic frame and content of K. B.'s theology are totally distinct from political reticence or irresponsibility; rather do they express the conviction that by its existence, constitution, proclamation and action the church itself is and has to be a political factor, even "church for the world," church for those changes in and of the world which correspond to God's kingdom.

V THE SUM OF THE MATTER

1. K. B.'s life and way, his academical work and his social engagement are the stuff out of which his theology is made. He produced a <u>Geschichts-Theologie</u> (a theology determined by and determinative for contemporary history) - though not in the sense of Joseph Hromadka who seemed to identify the finger of God with one particular form of social change. According to Marquardt, the anguish of preaching, the centrality of Jesus Christ, and the systematic ontological quest are incidental to the socio-historical core of Barthian theology.

2. Because throughout his life K. B. used two sources of authoritative information: the Bible and the newspaper, and because he devoted himself to two causes of equal prominence: the concept of God and the social condition, he ultimately did endorse the intention of "natural theology." Indeed, in <u>Theologische Existenz 1</u>, against the onrush of Nazism, K. B. coined the slogan, "doing theology as though nothing had happened." Admitted also that in the <u>Barmen Declaration,</u> as well as in his fight against (the Roman Catholic) Erich Przywara's and his former friend Emil Brunner's versions of natural theology, K. B. rebutted the theory of two sources of revelation. And yet, these were transitional outbursts which later were revoked in the light of K. B.'s Christological research, opines Marquardt.

3. Because God is the great revolutionary, and because K. B. sought to serve this God, Barthian theology can approprately be called a "theology of revolution." This theology is highly recommendable, and maybe indispensible, to all that hunger and thirst for social righteousness.

POLITICAL CHARACTER OF KARL BARTH'S THEOLOGY

VI THE FIRST EFFECTS OF MARQUARDT'S BOOK

Theologie und Sozialismus was submitted as Habilitationsschrift to the faculty of the Kirchliche Hochschule in West-Berlin. By a city-ordinance this equivalent of a church-related theological seminary was granted the de facto status of a theological faculty attached to the Freie Universität of the same city. After examination of the Marquardt manuscript, the faculty of the Kirchliche Hochschule graded the work as unscientific and refused to "habilitate" its author as a professor. Upon this, Helmut Gollwitzer resigned from his professorship at the same institution in order to devote his services exclusively to the Freie Universität. Soon after, Marquardt submitted his work to the Freie Universität where it was accepted and crowned with the author's appointment with professorial rank. Whether the legal steps taken by the Kirchliche Hochschule against this procedure will change anything, is not known at this moment.

2. Marquardt, adorned with a martyr's crown, became a hero to radical students and professors in Germany, as well as to many other groups in different parts of Europe. His lectures on the topic discussed in his book were attended by large crowds and hotly debated. Eduard Thurneysen was rushed to Berlin in order to clarify disputed points and serve as an arbiter. At any rate, through Marquardt, K. B. once more became a vital issue and his dusk-covered books were taken down from the shelves and re-opened. Especially "the young Barth" seemed ready for lionizing.

3. Some opponents of K. B.'s theology felt entitled to sneer, saying either, "I told you so, now we have the proof that K. B. was not only an incorrigible Swiss democrat, but even worse: also a Marxist," or, "K. B. has harvested what he has been sowing. After giving the devil the little finger, now he is taken in by him wholesale." On the other side, some so-called Barthians fell silent or cried out in disgust. Unlike Max Geiger in Berlin and H.-J. Kraus in Göttingen, the Tübingen professor E. Jüngel refused to give an evaluation of the book to the Habilitationsausschuss of the Freie Universität, and his retired colleague H. Diem wrote a scalding and devasting review in Evangelische Kommentare, exposing above all the ignorance, misunderstanding and misuse of Christology by Marquardt.

THE POLITICAL CHARACTER OF KARL BARTH'S THEOLOGY

4. In letters, small gatherings and public meetings, a spectre appeared on the wall: the split among the "Barthians" into right-wing and left-wing groups, analogous to the divisions separating <u>Rechts-</u> and <u>Links-Hegelianer</u>. Against the leftist radicals, a party of orthodox interpreters of K. B. appeared to be in process of formation, intent to save the light from the jaws of the communist serpent.

5. In order to discuss the issue, and if possible, to prevent the threatening split, a conference was arranged at which the problems could be discussed in open, thorough and friendly fashion. From July 10th - 14th, 1972, scholars and publishers who had volunteered to edit the post-humous K. B. works - materials for no less than 60 volumes, though not of the size of the <u>Church Dogmatics</u>, are available - met in the retreat center "Leuenberg" near Basel. After current editorial issues had been settled, the editors were joined by other interested and specifically competent parties, and two full days were devoted to the discussion of Marquardt's book.

VII HIGHLIGHTS OF A CONFERENCE

The Leuenberg Conference was convoked and presided by Professor Max Geiger. Professor Dieter Schellong of Münster, Westfalia, spoke on K. B.'s relationship to great issues of the 19th century. Eduard Thurneysen discussed - not without some substantial and pointed criticisms of Marquardt - the way of the early K. B. in the light of his complete correspondence with K. B. between 1913 and 1934, which will be published in 1973, and H. Diem re-iterated his observations on the use and misuse of Christology. During the intensive discussions it seemed as if the theologians present would indeed line up in two arrays, one side dominated by Helmut Gollwitzer and George Casalis, the other by Herrmann Diem and Eberhard Jüngel. However, there were also people who refused to participate in either a beatification or an anathematization of Marquardt - among them Frederick Herzog from Durham, North Carolina, and the professors Kreck, Geyer and Hübner from West-German universities. Scholars from behind the Iron Curtain were unable to attend the meeting.

In quick succession, three events exemplified the existing tension:

POLITICAL CHARACTER OF KARL BARTH'S THEOLOGY

1. Professor Casalis (of Paris) gave an unscheduled sermonic speech and said in substance the following: (a) Class struggle is the essence of all history; (b) God is never neutral in this struggle, for (c) he is always at the side of the proletariat and identifies himself with their cause; (d) therefore, only that man is a true theologian who is engaged in class struggle at the side of the poor and needy. At other occasions, Casalis had sought to undergird his stance by a kenotic form of Christology.

2. A discussion of Casalis' challenge was impossible because he spoke no earlier than at the end of a long evening discussion, immediately before his departure. Still, there was time enough for Professor Jüngel to stand straight up and declare, "In the freedom of the children of God of which Paul speaks in Rom. 8, I declare: <u>Ich bin ein Bürger</u>." The last words may indicate a democratic citizen's responsible position and procedure. However, after the Casalis oratory they sounded to some like a confession in favour of the bourgeois class.

3. Certainly they were understood in the latter sense by an American studying in Berlin who on the following morning addressed Professor Jüngel, "How could you, at this moment in history, take the side of the bourgeoisie? I doubt whether it is an exercise in freedom when you declare your solidarity with Nixon's disregard of the poor, the bombing of the dikes in North Vietnam, the belligerent attitude of the Christian Democratic Union in the <u>Bundesrepublik</u> against Mr. Brandt's reconciliatory <u>Ostpolitik</u>." Having heard this attack, E. Jüngel silently packed his brief-case, stood up and left the room, with just a little emphasis on the closing of the door behind him. It proved impossible to make him rejoin the meeting. Thus the "current discussion on the political character of K. B.'s theology" seemed to end in contempt and hatred, a deep abyss appeared to exist between actual or supposed followers of K. B. While earlier verbal exchanges at the conference had been less acerbated, they had been no less grave.

4. However, the conference was concluded neither with a bang nor a whimper. After extremists on both sides had had their say, more moderate voices began to be heard. The cause of the strife in person, F. W. Marquardt, declared his willingness to heed these voices, even at the expense of having to rewrite his book (which is at pre-

sent is out of print).

I wish to conclude my report by listing the most improtant contributions, as they were formulated especially by Professor Geyer of Bonn.

(a) In Marquardt's book, again and again historical observations and theories are converted into dogmatical affirmations. While recognizing that K. B. was not a system builder and did refuse both, to formulate a definitive concept of God and to endorse socialism and revolution as such, Marquardt has yet produced a theological-systematical theory. He might have learned from K. B.'s own excursions into the history of theology and the church that the formulation of dogmatical statements requires more than merely the reproduction of a picture of the past and present history. A new insight into the mystery of Jesus Christ himself, based on intensive Biblical studies, is indispensible whenever theology shall again become a liberating force.

(b) The tension Marquardt has constructed between an ontological and a dynamistic concept of God, that is, the alternative between the <u>esse</u> and the <u>operari</u> of God, and the search for the priority of the one or the other, appears to be inappropriate to the praise of God as proclaimed in K. B.'s works. Certainly, if God's nature (in K. B.'s terminology: his "perfection") is described by the terms "freedom" and "love", then neither a philosophical ontology nor an existentialistic dynamism, nor the harping upon the mutual exclusion of the two, can advance theological research and the church's witness.

(c) The use made by Marquardt of Christological arguments is foreign not only to their biblical basis and the historical setting of their discussion, but also to K. B.'s motivation and intention. Marquardt's contention that in K. B.'s theology Christology is no more than a subsidiary to, and confirmation of, preconceived ideas and experienced tensions is not at all convincing. Still, it must be admitted that the acrimonious debate about Christology at this conference has by no means brought to light what Jesus Christ really means for the poor, either in the Bible or in K. B.'s exposition of the Bible.

(d) Even if it would make good sense to call God the arch-revolutionary and his kingdom the true revolution for the benefit of all the world, Marquardt has not yet shown to what change "revolution" is subjected once it is taken into Yahweh's and Jesus Christ's hands. Certainly God and Christ do more than merely confirm and endorse one brand of radical political and social thought and action.

Observations, questions and suggestions such as these formed the highlights of the Leuenberg conference. For the time being, they prevented the threatening split into rival factions. They appeared to imply that Marquardt has put his finger upon an essential element of K. B.'s theology: God's revelation in the incarnate *logos* proves how totally God himself cares for the whole human condition, including all the material and social issues. Revelation by incarnation also demonstrates that theology, together with every other feature of the church's life and witness, cannot help but be political, whenever it is faithful to God. However, the questions posed also included a very critical assessment of the methods and arguments chosen by Marquardt. Above all they showed that K. B.'s heritage requires hard, courageous and productive future work. Instead of giving pat answers it urges the whole church to speak even better and clearer of him who was in Christ reconciling the world.

MICHAEL WYSCHOGROD

Why Was and Is the Theology of Karl Barth of Interest to a Jewish Theologian?

I have been asked to explain why a Jewish theologian is interested in the work of Karl Barth. Implied in that question is a more generic one: why is a Jewish theologian interested in Christianity and Christian theology? Let us therefore start with the genus and then turn to the species.

Since every question proceeds from a frame of reference and is based on some assumptions, it is reasonable to assume that the asking of this question proceeds from some degree of wonder that a Jewish theologian should be interested in Christianity. It has been argued, and there are those who continue to maintain, that while an interest in Judaism is necessary and inevitable for the Christian theologian, a corresponding interest in Christianity is neither necessary nor inevitable for the Jewish theologian. Christianity, we are reminded, presupposes Judaism from which it originated and whose promises it claims to have fulfilled. As such, a knowledge of Judaism is essential for a Christian who wishes to understand his faith. Judaism, the argument continues, does not presuppose Christianity and can therefore pursue its path without much interest in Christianity. While it is, of course, a fact of life that Judaism has, for much of its history, existed in a Christian world and, therefore, been forced into contact with Christian civilization, those who believe that an interest in Christianity is not essential to Judaism consider this relationship a relatively external one, not reaching into the religious center of Jewish faith. It is on such ground that the mild wonder aroused by a Jewish theologian who nevertheless is interested in Christian theology can perhaps be explained. Furthermore, there is the degree of strain that has obtained between the two faiths for some time, a strain that you probably have heard of, and that, too, enters the calculation when this question is considered. In the light of all this, why is a Jewish theologian interested in Christianity? What explains this mystery?

It is, of course, not possible to deny the validity

A JEWISH THEOLOGIAN AND KARL BARTH

of the point concerning the a-symmetry between Judaism and Christianity as regarding their origins. Christianity is rooted in Judaism in a way that Judaism is not rooted in Christianity and there seems to be no way of escaping this fact. I cannot, however, conclude from this that a Jewish theologian, therefore, ought or perhaps even must remain uninterested in Christianity. I base this opinion on two considerations, both of which, I think, bear attention by Jewish theology.

First, there is the Divine promise to Abraham that through his election, or in him, there shall be blessed the families of the earth (Gen. 12:3). This makes quite clear that the election of Abraham and his seed, while in many ways separating the history of Israel from those of the nations, cannot rest with such a separation. However appropriate such a separation may be on the way, in a fundamental sense the destinies of the families of the earth and that of Israel are intertwined because it is the Divine intention that the blessing which is initially Abraham's, in time redound to the benefit of the nations. Israel cannot therefore be ultimately isolationist, however vital it be that it be so penultimately. As it pursues its path through history, it expects the redemption of the nations and watches with great interest those developments which give indication of such a future. Because this is so, the Jewish theologian can and must maintain a vital interest in the spiritual life of the nations with whom it is, in a sense, jointly embarked on the path to redemption. It is not to detract from the centrality assigned to Israel in this process to emphasize this point. Not to emphasize it is too often symptomatic of a misunderstanding of Israel's election, as if the redemption of Israel could be accomplished alongside the non-redemption of the nations.

But if the Jewish theologian is therefore necessarily interested in the religious life of all peoples, how much more must he be interested in Christianity which has mediated the vocabulary of Israel to all parts of the earth. At times, I find myself driving on a Sunday morning in some rural area of the United States. At this time, as one plays with the dial on the car radio, just about the only reception available consists of church services from this or that local church. And as one switches from station to station, what names does one hear? David, Solomon, Ezekiel, Jeremiah, Isaiah,

A JEWISH THEOLOGIAN AND KARL BARTH

Jesus, Paul and so on, Jews one and all. And what concepts does one hear? Sin and redemption, the Messiah, sacrifice, the Passover, Jerusalem and so on, Jewish concepts one and all. And this Jewish vocabulary, this imagination, these Jewish hopes and expectations issue from gentile seed, from stock that is not of Abraham, from people whose forefathers had not been brought out of Egypt and for whom God did not split the Red Sea. How can a Jewish theologian not be interested in this? True, to the Jewish ear there are at times notes that are not fully harmonious with his consciousness, notes often disturbing and even strange. But it is not this that is the wonder. The wonder is that nations not of the stock of Abraham have come within the orbit of the faith of Israel, experiencing man and history with Jewish categories deeply rooted in Jewish experience and sensibility. How can a Jewish theologian not perceive that something wonderful is at work here, something that must in some way be connected with the love of the God of Israel for all his children, Isaac as well as Ishmael, Jacob as well as Esau. It is this that Maimonides perceived about Christianity when he wrote that Jesus "only served to clear the way for King Messiah, to prepare the whole world to worship God with one accord, as it is written 'For then will I turn to the people a pure language, that they may all call upon the name of the lord to serve Him with one consent'(Zeph.3:9). Thus the messianic hope, the Torah, and the commandments have become familiar topics - topics of conversation (among the inhabitants) of the far isles and many peoples...."[1] Because Christianity has and continues to play this crucial role related to Israel's mission, Jewish theology cannot fail to be interested in Christian developments.

My second reason for believing that Judaism should cultivate an interest in Christian theology is perhaps less central than the first but nevertheless important. Christianity is heir to an exceedingly rich theological tradition. For various reasons, Judaism has not generally invested its most active energies in the theological enterprise. In order to interpret this fact correctly, considerable acquaintance with Christian theology is required. In the process, the Jewish theologian learns better to understand the framework of his faith because he compares it with an alternate strategy, one

A JEWISH THEOLOGIAN AND KARL BARTH

that was not taken by his tradition. The result is that dialogue with a theology as sophisticated as that of Christianity advances Judaism theologically and compels it to examine problems it might not otherwise have done. The danger in all this is that Judaism, by being forced into a theological mold perhaps partially foreign to it, is moved toward a self-understanding that is defective in proportion to its exchange of immediacy for mediacy, of being for doctrine, of life for thought and of the Scriptural for the philosophic. But no advance is possible without risk and it should be possible for a responsible Jewish theology to benefit from the experience of Christian theology and avoid those pitfalls so clearly marked out by Barth.

Having made these points in defense of a Jewish theologian's interest in Christian theology generally, it is now necessary to focus on Karl Barth and to ask why he, in particular, attracts the attention of a Jewish theologian? The answer can be stated very simply. Karl Barth is the Christian theologian of our time who is oriented toward Scripture, who does not substitute the Word of Man for that of God and who does not find himself helpless before the mighty technology of "scientific" Biblical scholarship - an enterprise often replete will all sorts of hidden agendas not obvious at first sight. And because Barth is Scriptural, his attention turns to Israel in a rather unique way which the Jewish theologian reads with avid interest if for no other reason than the feeling that it was not written to be read by a Jew, to be commented on by a Jew, to be challenged by a Jew. It cannot, of course, be maintained that this is unique with Barth. Bultmann, to mention but one other example, is at least equally oblivious to the possibility of falling into Jewish hands. But then he is so thoroughly gentile, so Heideggerian, so little humbled by the so largely Jewish Word of God, that one would not expect much from him. Barth is different. Because he is so biblical he is, in some sense, a member of the family whom Israel cannot ignore.

The first and basic point then that impresses a Jewish reader of Barth is that his faith is not grounded in some alleged eternal verities of reason or on some noble and profound religious sensibility that is shared by all men or by a spiritual elite, but on a movement of God toward man as witnessed in Scripture. It is of

A JEWISH THEOLOGIAN AND KARL BARTH

course true that in this formulation we have omitted the Christological center without which any summation of Barth's position is incomplete, to say the very least. For him, God's movement toward man is inconceivable without Jesus and it is he who is witnessed in Scripture. The Jewish reader, however, while fully realizing the centrality of the Christological in Barth, can understand Barth's appreciation of God's movement toward man in the light of the Word of God which, after all, is also central for Barth, even if not fully equal to the event of Jesus. The two concepts that emerge as crucial are therefore the theology of divine initiative and the theology of the word, both of which are deeply Barthian.

Both of these points are Jewish points. It is Israel that speaks of its God as He who has brought it out of Egypt and entered into covenant with this people. It is not inaccurate to say that Israel's definition of God is derived from the saving acts experienced by Israel at the hands of this God. The God of Israel is therefore the God of Abraham, Isaac and Jacob from which it follows that the God spoken of without the explicit or implicit invocation of the patriarchs is, to Israel, a foreign God who does not simply automatically coincide with its God. Barth's refusal to substitute ontological constructions, whether in the form of the "ground of being" or any other similar deflection of the God known by Israel, for the God who acts in Jewish history, cannot fail to meet with instinctive recognition by the Jewish reader that he has before him a biblically attuned thinker whose focus is on the God of Israel, even if, at a certain point, the Jewish story diverges from the Christian. I am convinced that it is necessary to formulate the matter in these terms, to speak of stories that diverge, because too often rationalistically minded Jewish theologians have made it appear that Judaism resists incarnation on some _a priori_ grounds as if the Jewish philosopher can somehow determine ahead of time just what God can or cannot do, what is or is not possible for Him, what His dignity does or does not allow. The truth is, of course, that it would be difficult to imagine anything further removed from authentic Jewish faith which does not prescribe for God from some alien frame of reference but listens obediently to God's free decisions, none of which can be prescribed or even anticipated by man. If Judaism cannot accept incarnation it

A JEWISH THEOLOGIAN AND KARL BARTH

is because it does not hear this story, because the Word of God as it hears it does not tell it and because Jewish faith does not testify to it. And if the church does accept incarnation, it is not because it somehow discovered that such an event had to occur given the nature of God, or of being, reality, or anything else, but because it hears that this was God's free and gracious decision, a decision not predictable by man. Strangely enough, the disagreement between Judaism and Christianity, when understood in this light, while not reconcilable, can be brought into the context within which it is a difference of faith regarding the free and sovereign act of the God of Israel.

Barth's relation to Scripture is the second point at which the Jewish reader senses a kinship that is crucial. Barthian theology is obedient listening to the Word of God. Barth develops his theology of Scripture in the early volumes of the Dogmatics and while it can hardly be maintained that Scripture diminishes in significance in the later volumes, it nevertheless seems that after the initial discussion Barth does not reopen this basic issue. In any case, Barth knows what Scriptural authority is, and is constitutionally incapable of imposing on the Word of God hermeneutic devices derived from alien loyalties which so often, in other cases, turn out to be Greek or other gentile sensibilities. The loyalty to the Scriptural is therefore a spiritual conversion to Israel's mind, a matter of decisive significance. That Barth is the first Christian theologian to look to Scripture for his foundation would be impossible to maintain. Luther and Calvin were also, of course, Scriptural in a very fundamental way. And yet, there is a difference. Strangely enough, perhaps it is the historical perspective that any writer in the twentieth century, even one as resistant to historical relativization as Barth, brings to his work. For Luther and Calvin it was probably not altogether clear that the Bible was an ancient document which must be read by means of an attempt to penetrate the minds of the ancient Jews to whom the Word of God was addressed. Barth is not primarily a historian; Bible-centered as he is, he is not a Hebrew scholar (his Greek and Latin are clearly superior to his Hebrew, unfortunately) and he does not capitalize on the latest advances in "scientific" biblical scholarship. Nevertheless, there is a very clear recognition of the dis-

A JEWISH THEOLOGIAN AND KARL BARTH

tance in space and time between Jerusalem and Basel and
the result of this is that Barth does not carry as much
of his Swiss identity into his work as might otherwise
have been the case. Consciousness of the historical
alone is not sufficient for the achievement of this
attachment to a God who has, as it were, hyphenated his
name to that of Israel so that the two move through history together. This is proven by Bultmann who, historian that he is, also remains splendidly gentile to an
amazing extent. But Barth, I think, does not remain a
gentile, which is to say, he becomes a Christian.

All of this must not, however, be taken to mean that
Barth's relation to the written Word of God is the
same as that of Judaism. Because he is, in a sense, so
close to it that his distance from it is so apparent.
I know of no better way of illustrating this than by
reference to the so-called Law, the commandments of the
Pentateuch which are the foundations of Judaism. It is
not necessary here to review the Law-Gospel problem in
Luther, Calvin and its appropriation by Barth. After
all the complexity of this issue is taken into account,
after we survey the fulfillment of the Law in Gospel
which is so central to Christianity, the fact still remains that the commandments of the Pentateuch remain
standing, the "moral" as well as the "ritual", and Israel is told time and again that they are to remain
"unto all your generations." Because Israel hears the
Word of God in Scripture it is simply not capable of
dismissing these commandments, whether they make sense
or whether they do not, whether they are in the domain
of morality or even conflict with human morality. Immanuel Kant, in commentating on Psalm 59, 11-14 in
which he finds "a prayer for revenge which goes to terrifying extremes" can dismiss with contempt a writer
who comments "The Psalms are inspired; if in them
punishment is prayed for, it cannot be wrong, and we
must have no morality holier than the Bible" and instead hurl the following rhetorical question which,
for Kant, obviously settles the issue: "I raise the
question as to whether morality should be expounded
according to the Bible or whether the Bible should not
rather be expounded according to morality."[2] Expounding the Bible according to morality, the choice of
Kant, is surely the antithesis of everything Barth believes, a form of natural ethics corresponding to that

other error, natural theology. The Jewish reader
therefore dreams of a Barth who would understand Israel's
refusal to discard its commandments, its stubborn clinging to practices which make no sense other than that
they are written in the Bible which is all we know or
need to know. I have not found in Barth such an understanding of Israel's biblical obedience. Upon more so-
ber reflection, however, that too is understandable.

We must return to Christology. Barth is profoundly
right when he emphasizes so often that the glory of his
God is his making himself humble enough to enter into
intercourse with man. This is the most amazing proclamation of the Hebrew Bible, the decisive difference
that separates it from the Platonic and the Aristote-
lian Godhead. As such, the Christian proclamation that
God became man in the person of Jesus of Nazareth is
but a development of the basic thrust of the Hebrew
Bible, God's movement toward man. And if all this is
true, then at least in this respect, the difference between Judaism and Christianity is one of degree rather
than kind. Nevertheless, even here a difference remains. Without the incarnation, however much movement
towards man there is on the part of God, there remains
a separation between them which is decisive. If God
became man, the gulf is really bridged, the natures
joined if not fused, the incommensurable made commensurable. And if this is so, there can be no demand
made on man which is alien to his nature, in which
God's demand cuts into the flesh of man because it
comes from Him who is other than man, who, while gra-
ciously having entered into relation with man, is
nevertheless not man but God. The God who became man
commands a being who at least once was fused with God,
which destroyed once and for all the abyss between
them. Israel can therefore tolerate a command which it
cannot understand just because it comes from God who is
not one with man. From Israel's vantage point, the divine command must both reverberate in man's being and
appear strange to him because God has turned to man
but it is also different from him. It is therefore almost necessary, if I may be permitted a forbidden word,
that the divine commandments on the one hand fulfill
Israel's deepest moral being and on the other also sha-
tter it, because God is not man. To the Jewish reader,
it is difficult to escape the feeling that in Christ-

ianity there is a tendency toward the rationalization of the commandments, though the word "rationalization" might not be the best possible. In any case, it is a tendency to make the commandments spiritually comprehensible as in Jesus' contention that (Mark 2:27) "The sabbath was made for man, and not man for the sabbath," a remark which directs attention to the recipient of the sabbath rather than to its originator. For the Jew, while the sabbath was given to Israel, it is commanded by God who is not commensurable with man and whose demands need not always "make sense" to man. In fact, any system of demands which fully made sense to man might likely be the work of his hands rather than the Word of God. It seems to me, therefore, that in this respect Judaism is more Barthian than Barth - a possibility that, I hope, will not strike you as just too funny.

The proximity and distance between Israel and God is expressed most forcefully in rabbinic literature in the duality of God's attributes of Law (Din) and Mercy (Rachamim). At times God acts in accordance with law, as the judge who metes out to each what he deserves. At other times he acts in accordance with mercy, cancelling deserved condemnation and awarding undeserved rewards. The Jew is fully aware that no man can pass muster before God if he rests his case on law, on what he deserves, rather than the unmerited mercy of God. "Not because of our righteousness," explains the daily morning liturgy, "do we lay our supplication before thee, but because of thine abundant mercies." Paul's polemic against justification by law is therefore hardly an attack on Judaism, as if the Jew felt no need for the mercy of God but rested his case on what was coming to him under the law! No thought could be more alien to Israel. Without God's mercy man is hopelessly lost in his sin, in his guilt before God. But while God's mercy can be beseeched, it cannot be guaranteed because, however terrible for man to contemplate, at times God does mete out justice. If mercy corresponds to God's proximity and law to his remoteness, then Judaism sees an alternation which it cannot control. True, in some ultimate sense God's mercy exceeds his justice, his reconciliation with Israel will be forever while his remoteness is only temporary. But in the pre-redeemed time the wrath of God is felt by Israel as the deserved chastisement of the people whom God loves above all others.

For Christianity, things are otherwise. Before Christ, Paul seems to think, there was law and mercy and one could never know which would rule at any given moment. If anything, it was law that predominated. With the coming of Christ, there is a permanent and fundamental change. Jesus is equated with the divine attribute of mercy so that those who believe in him, permanently escape the danger of standing in the relationship of law to God. In Christ, the attribute of mercy (Midas Horachamim) has once and for all triumphed which means that the believer has now escaped the possibility of encountering the justice of God, of being judged according to the law, according to what he deserves. The Christological event is therefore the final drawing together of God and man, their final reconciliation.

In the later volumes of the Dogmatics, this reconciliation also triumphs in the theology of Barth. His divergence from Calvin in the rigors of predestination is rooted in the reconciliation that is the event of Jesus Christ. And just as the proximity to God erased those features of the law that were incommensurable with the understanding of man, so the proximity to God, the incarnation, makes possible the triumph of mercy and the permanent calming of the fear of those who, while praying for the mercy of God, know that God is sovereign, that His love cannot be fathomed by man and that therefore His wrath, His deserved wrath, cannot be excluded as a possibility. I have often wondered why the House of Israel whose intimacy with the God of Abraham cannot, after all, be paralleled by any other people, can live with this proximity and remoteness, this possibility of wrath together with the certainty of love, while the gentiles who draw near to the God of Abraham cannot bear his wrath, only his more fundamental love. Perhaps the answer is that toward the natural son, the father can afford to lose his temper because there is a security that cannot be shaken. The adopted son must be dealt with more carefully, with greater love, because there is less security, less certainty of the love of the father, a lingering remoteness that must be fought by a greater proximity. If this is so, then the wrath of God is Israel's sign

A JEWISH THEOLOGIAN AND KARL BARTH

of sonship, of its being the first-born, the caressed son of election. But the gentiles in Christ are also loved and in time will also be worthy of his wrath.

It is now possible to turn to the final topic that requires discussion if you are to understand at all why a Jew is interested in Karl Barth. I am referring to his doctrine of Israel, a topic dealt with at some length by Marquardt in his recent study.[3] Given Barth's attention to Scripture, given his refusal to substitute human theorizing for the Word of God, it is inevitable that the Jewish people and Judaism play a significant role in his theology because they do in Scripture, both in the Old and New Testaments. But this, of course, is hardly unexpected or new. Christian authors from the very first have been interested in Judaism. What is decisive about Barth is his insight into the status of the Jewish people after the decisive event of their rejection of the Messiahship of Jesus of Nazareth. Very often, the view explicitly or implicitly held was that, while the Jews had been the chosen people up until Christ, once they rejected the messiah who had been sent to them, they lost their election and their place was taken by the church which thus became the "new Israel", a phrase used as recently as Vatican II to describe the church. This view Barth apparently rejected decisively. In 1949 he wrote: "Without any doubt the Jews are to this very day the chosen people of God in the same sense as they have been so from the beginning, according to the Old and New Testaments. They have the promise of God; and if we Christians from among the Gentiles have it too, then it is only as those chosen with them; as guests in their house, as new wood grafted onto their old tree."[4] In 1942, while the Jews of Europe were being murdered by the millions in Europe, he wrote: "A Church that becomes antisemitic or even only a-semitic sooner or later suffers the loss of its faith by loosing the object of it."[5] And again, speaking of Israel, he writes: "For it is incontestable that this people as such is the holy people of God: the people with whom God has dealt in His grace and in His wrath; in the midst of whom He has blessed and judged, enlightened and hardened, accepted and rejected; whose cause either way He has made His own, and has not ceased to make His own, and will not cease to make His own. They are all of them by nature sanctified by Him,

A JEWISH THEOLOGIAN AND KARL BARTH

sanctified as ancestors and kinsmen of the Holy One in Israel, in a sense that Gentiles are not by nature, not even the best of Gentiles, not even the Gentile Christians, not even the best of Gentile Christians, in spite of their membership of the Church, in spite of the fact that they too are now sanctified by the Holy One of Israel and have become Israel."[6] It may be an exaggeration to assert that statements such as these cannot be found in the writings of any other contemporary Christian theologians. But if they exist, they cannot easily be found and, in any case, are probably not as clear as those of Barth. Barth is thus perfectly clear about the election of the Jewish people, especially their continuing election after the crucifixion. It will hardly surprise you to learn that this is pleasing to a Jewish reader who sees in this a Christian return to its roots in the faith of Israel.

But this, of course, is not the whole story. Together with statements such as those just referred to, are others more conventionally Christian and less pleasing to the Jewish reader. Marquardt draws some of those phrases together from the exposition in Paragraph #34 of the <u>Dogmatics</u> in a sentence all of whose operative phrases are quotations from Barth's discussion of Jews and Judaism in this key portion of the <u>Dogmatics</u>:"Barth sagt von der Synagoge in #34, sie sei die "ungeheure Schattenseite der Geschichte Israels", das "ungehorsame, götzendienerische Israel aller Zeiten", das "nur durch Gottes Zorn geheiligte Israel zur Linken", sei die "Synagoge des Todes", die zwar "hörende, aber bei allem ihrem Hören immer noch glaubenslose Synagoge"; sie sei die "tragische, unheimlich schmerzliche Gestalt mit verbundenen Augen", sei "leibhaftig das in Erstarrung stehen gebliebene Alte Testament an sich und in abstracto", sei die "Organisation einer noch und noch in eine leere Zukunft eilenden Menschheit"; sie biete das "Phänomen der ungläubigen", das "Phänomen der renitenten Synagoge", sei charakterisiert von "hochmütiger Lüge" und ihrem "nationalistisch-gesetzlichen Messiastraum"; sie biete schlechthin eine "gespensterhafte Gestalt"; ihre Mitglieder seien "unselige Mitglieder der Synagoge" und "die Synagogenjuden gehören nicht zu den Gehorsamen"; es sei die Synagoge "das unecht gewordene Israel", sie stehe da "als Feind Gottes", habe "an der

A JEWISH THEOLOGIAN AND KARL BARTH

Erfüllung der ihr gegebenen Verheissung zunächst keinen Anteil", habe eine "trostlose Zeitrechnung", lebe eine "Fleischliche Hoffnung", realisiere eine "fleischliche Treue gegen sich selbst", praktiziere "jüdischen Starrsinn, Trübsinn, Schrulle, Phantasterei" - kurz: sie biete das Bild einer "halb ehrwürdigen, halb grausigen Reliquie, einer wunderlich konservativen Antiquität", das Bild "menschlicher Schrulle".[7] While it is true, as Marquardt himself admits, that the very drawing together of all these expressions in one sentence lifts them from their context and conveys a somewhat more negative picture than is warranted, the fact remains that Barth uses every one of these expressions in that paragraph and that no complete account of Barth's position on Judaism can be even provisionally complete without taking this fact into account. What is to be made of it?

The truth is that Barth's position towards Jews is ambivalent. Because of the authenticity of his Christianity, because he reads Scripture obediently, he becomes aware of the centrality of Israel in God's relation with man and in the very message that Christianity proclaims to the world. There is little doubt that Barth's experience with Nazism taught him just how equivalent the anti-Christ is to anti-semitism, how necessary the destruction of the Jewish people is to those who make war on the God of Israel and his commandments. But there is also in Barth an anti-semitism made up of two parts: the traditional anti-semitism of European Christiandom (whether the Swiss suffer from this more or less than others I cannot say) and the anti-semitism of Christian theology. As far as the first sort of anti-semitism is concerned, it may surprise some that a man of Barth's stature is not completely immune to it. But we must never forget that Barth is also a human being subject to human frailties. In this connection, I have wondered for years how a man whom I admire as much as I do Karl Barth, with near-perfection of his grasp of the evil of Nazism, could have had less than a perfect grasp of the evil of that other great war on the God of Israel, Communism. The only answer I have been able to come up with is that it was God's way of reminding us that Karl Barth, after all, was only a human being. The rabbis claim that the reason that the burial place of Moses was not made known was the

A JEWISH THEOLOGIAN AND KARL BARTH

fear that, were it known, it might have become a focus of worship, with the concomitant danger that divine attributes would have been attached to Moses. With Karl Barth, too, in the absence of one relatively major flaw, there is no knowing what people would have made of him. It is perhaps for this reason that the vision in his left eye was not permitted to be equal to that in his right.

Putting aside the less prominent portion of Barth's defective attitude to Judaism, the conventionally European one, we must turn to the far more important aspect, the theological one. Here the crux of the matter is, of course, Israel's rejection of the messiahship of him who is the Lord of the church. This is a decisive matter and it would be ludicrous to minimize the significance of this rejection. In fact, I find it interesting that the church concluded that, in spite of the fact that a minority of Jews accepted Jesus as the Christ, it was not this minority that represented the Jewish people, but the non-accepting majority that did so. Barth, in close conformity to the tradition, detects a pattern here. Israel, the elect people, is also from the very first a rebellious people who kills its prophets, etc. The rejection of Jesus is therefore very much in character for the Jews who are established experts in returning disobedience for the unmerited gifts that God bestows on this people. Again and again we are told that the record of Israel is consistent: to return evil for the good of God, disobedience for love, rebellion for faithfulness.

We have reached a point where I have one confession and one comment to make. The confession is simply this: there is nothing more important that I have learned from Barth than the sinfulness of Israel. There is no question that the history of the Jewish people is a history of obduracy and of unfaithfulness. It is a people that, time and again, has returned evil for God's good and has suffered grievously for it. I do not know that this point would be as clear in my mind were it not for my reading of Barth (and of course, Paul). It might be surprising that this should require a reading of Barth when this point is so clear in the Bible. Nevertheless, it is not a point which is naturally in the forefront of Jewish consciousness and I am deeply grateful to Barth for teaching it to me.

A JEWISH THEOLOGIAN AND KARL BARTH

But, to turn from confession to comment, it is not the whole truth. Reading Barth, one would gain the impression that there is nothing but faithfulness on God's part and unfaithfulness on Israel's. This is not so. "Go and cry in the ears of Jerusalem," proclaims Jeremiah (2:23), "saying, Thus saith the Lord: I remember thee, the kindness of thy youth, the love of thine espousals, when thou wentest after me in the wilderness, in a land that was not sown. Israel is holiness unto the Lord, and the first fruits of his increase, all that devour him shall offend; evil shall come upon them, saith the Lord." There is nothing but faithfulness on God's part but it is not the case that there is nothing but unfaithfulness on Israel's part. Along with the unfaithfulness, there is also Israel's faithfulness, its obedience and trust in God, its clinging to its election, identity and mission against all the odds. True, all of Israel's obedience is tinged with its disobedience but all of its disobedience is also tinged with its obedience. It is true that Israel does not deserve its election but it is also true that its election is not in vain, that this people, with its sin, has never ceased to love its God and that it has responded to God's wrath, to his unspeakable wrath, to his unthinkable wrath, by shouldering its mission again, again searing circumcision into its flesh and, while hoping for the best, prepared for what it knows can happen again. Perhaps it is not seemly to speak thus, to praise Israel when it should be criticized. But he who knows the God of Israel knows how he loves his people and that he loves those who love it.

To see Barth struggling toward the sign that is Israel, to see him fighting against his Gentile nature that demands antipathy to the people of election, to see this nature yield to the Word of God and to Barth's love for that Jew whom he loves above all others, is to see the miraculous work of God. The work is incomplete. There remains a dark side, an emphasis on Israel's disobedience which, as we have said, is not the whole truth. But even more important is this final point. Whatever Israel's problems with its God may be, however great Israel's sin and God's wrath may be, the quarrel is a family one, between Israel and its God, its father. For strangers to intervene, to point out the shortcomings of the son, to revel in them, to make

A JEWISH THEOLOGIAN AND KARL BARTH

a theology of them, to feel superior because of them, is a very, very dangerous strategy. However terrible the anger of a father toward his son may be, it is an anger that he can afford because underneath it is a love that is a father's. When others are stimulated by this anger, something totally different enters the picture and the father can only be appalled. It is very dangerous to get mixed up in such family quarrels. He who does, will incur the wrath of both sides.

I will therefore be frank. It is not for gentiles, to see the sins of Israel. It is not for gentiles to call Israel to its mission, to feel morally superior to it and to play the prophets role towards it. It is for gentiles to love this people if need be blindly, staunchly, not impartially but partially and to trust the instincts of this people whom God has chosen as His own. If they need be chastized they will be, by their father who is not fooled. But woe unto those gentiles who become the rod of God's chastisement of Israel, the instrument of this anger, the satisfied by-standers of the punishment. It were better had they not been born rather than witness this lovers' quarrel.

I have said that it is for gentiles to love Israel. This, of course, is wrong, it cannot be asked of gentiles. But it can be asked of Christians.

NOTES

1 The Code of Maimonides Book Fourteen The Book of Judges tr. Abraham M. Hershman (New Have, Yale, 1949) p XXIII
2 Immanuel Kant Religion Within the Limits of Reason Alone tr. Greene and Hudson (New York, Harper and Row, 1960) p 101
3 Friedrich-Wilhelm Marquardt Die Entdeckung des Judentums für die christliche Theologie: Israel in Denken Karl Barths (München, Kaiser Verlag, 1967)
4 Karl Barth "The Jewish Problem and the Christian Answer" in Against the Stream (London, SCM Press, 1954) p 200
5 Karl Barth Church Dogmatics II 2 p 234
6 Ibid, p 287
7 Marquardt p 335. In paragraph 34 of the CD, Barth refers to the Synagogue as 'that dark and monstrous side of Israel's history', 'the disobedient, idola-

A JEWISH THEOLOGIAN AND KARL BARTH

trous Israel of every age', 'the whole of Israel on the
left hand, sanctified only by God's wrath'; he says that
the Synagogue is 'the Synagogue of death' which, yes,
'hears the Word and yet for and in all its hearing is
still unbelieving', is 'the tragic, terribly painful
figure with covered eyes', the 'living petrification of
the Old Testament in itself and in abstracto', an 'organization of a humanity which again and again hastens
toward an empty future'. That organization, Barth states,
is 'the phenomenon of the unbelieving, the refractory
Synagogue', which is characterized by a 'vaunting lie'
and its 'nationalistic-legalistic Messiah-dream', it stands
there like a 'spectral form', its members are 'wretched
members of the Synagogue'; 'the Synagogue Jews are not
numbered among the obedient'. Rather, the Synagogue is
'the debased Israel of the Synagogue', it is seen as 'an
enemy of God', which has 'no....part now in the fulfilment of the promise given to it', going by a 'cheerless
chronology', living a 'carnal hope', taking a stand on
'a carnal loyalty to itself', and practicing 'Jewish
obduracy, melancholy, caprice and phantasy' - in short,
the Synagogue cuts the figure of 'a half-venerable, half-
gruesome relic, of a miraculously preserved antique', the
figure of 'human whimsicality.' (II/2 195ff).

EMILIEN LAMIRANDE

The Impact of Karl Barth on the Catholic Church in the Last Half Century

To my knowledge it is the Dutch Dominican B. A. Willems who, in his small but useful book: Karl Barth. An Ecumenical Approach to his Theology, comes nearest to a general evaluation of Barth's impact on the Christian world.[1] A few particular aspects of the relationship between Barth and Roman Catholicism have been carefully examined. Henri Bouillard has studied the attitude of Barth towards the Roman Church in a very perceptive essay published in 1970.[2] Grover Foley has analyzed with deep insight the Catholic reaction from the theological point of view.[3] My approach, I admit, is different, and as an historian of Christian doctrine rather than as a theologian, I am equally concerned with some of the quantitative aspects as with the qualitative dimension of Barth's impact on Roman Catholicism.

(1) THE IMPACT OF BARTH ON ROMAN CATHOLICISM

Since it is through Hans Küng that Catholic theology was afforded a voice, in 1968, at the funeral of Barth, in Basel, I will take his tribute as a starting point for my address. After mentioning that he had been allowed for the last 15 years to regard Barth as his fatherly friend and constant spiritual companion, Küng alluded to Barth's one time tempestuous relationship with Roman Catholicism: "This may be surprising when we consider that hardly one important theologian of our century has attacked the Catholic Church and Catholic theology as positively, as angrily, and as defiantly as has Karl Barth - in his Church Dogmatics as surely as at the General Assembly of the World Council of Churches in Amsterdam....But his challenge was set forth for all its polemic with that quality which he so praised in Mozart - a great, passionate, free objectivity. And the subject for which he wished to obtain a hearing - a wide hearing - was the Christian message. With the gospel as his starting point, he believed it necessary to speak so sharply, he believed it necessary to protest against us. And he seemed to many of us to be the Protestant theologian par excellence. But actually he protested

BARTH'S IMPACT ON THE CATHOLIC CHURCH

not only when he was against something but when he was for something ..."4

Barth protested for the wholly other living God, for the ever relevant Word of God in Scripture, for the centrality of Jesus Christ, for the community of believing men and because of that he has made again Protestant theology a partner for Roman Catholicism. This is a momentous affirmation that we may like to hear attentively in Küng's own words: "With his positive protest, his great evangelical intentions, which must be maintained throughout, no matter what one's position regarding the Barthian system, Karl Barth has again made Protestant theology itself an earnest, evangelical discussion partner for us Catholics. And with this protest he has at the same time awakened many of us Catholics. His prophetic word, also in the Dogmatics, was heard in our church too, and he himself was surprised how well heard it was. Karl Barth, precisely as a fundamentally evangelical theologian in his influence even on the Catholic Church - very indirect and yet very effective (and to say this is no exaggeration) - has become one of the spiritual fathers of the Catholic renewal in connection with the Second Vatican Council, a renewal which in most recent years often permitted him to ask with mixed feeling of sadness and joy whether the Spirit of God was not as much alive in the Catholic Church as in his own."5

I will borrow from these moving comments the main theme of my address. With Barth, Protestant theology had been made again - perhaps for the first time since the XVIth Century - an authentic discussion partner for Roman Catholics.6 Keeping in mind the term impact which somewhat includes the idea of influence, but is wider in comprehension, we will ask three questions in connection with the fact that Karl Barth has elicited a tremendous Catholic response: Why did it happen at all?, How did it happen?, and With which results for the Roman Catholic Church? Before we examine separately each of these questions, let us acquaint ourselves briefly with the very existence of an impact of Barth on Catholicism.

In his lively portrait of Barth, Georges Casalis, states that not since Luther and Calvin did Protestantism have a single theologian of the stature and importance of Karl Barth, by whose message the Reformed Churches have been literally shaken. He goes on underlining the different impact it had on Roman Catholicism: "The Reformed churches have been so utterly shaken by Barth's message, and the reverberations of his work within those churches have been so far-reaching, that they have not yet adjusted themselves to the new situation. ⁕ Like a patient who recovers his health very slowly after a critical operation, they are incapable of analyzing what has happened and of taking their bearings. Paradoxically - or perhaps very naturally if the comparison holds - those who are strangers to the Protestant ethos, for the most part Roman Catholics, have been much more concerned about Barth's impact and its implications. The list of works published by them is increasing all the time, and already includes a number of works of considerable importance, making clear that Barth is watched, listened to and understood with real penetration by those outside the circle of his own confession (he belongs to the Calvinist wing of the Reformed church), as well as by the larger group of churches coming from the Reformation itself."[7] And Casalis adds a little farther: "If von Balthasar is right, not only is Protestantism renewed in the process, but the whole church is likewise affected..."[8]

Karl Barth himself in one of his contributions to the Christian Century comments upon the decade 1948-1958: "A special word is necessary concerning what has happened in the encounter between Roman Catholic theology and myself. Whatever a man may think about me otherwise, he will have to grant me the strange fame entailed in the fact that since the Reformation no figure in Protestant theology has aroused so much critical but also positive and in any case serious interest on the part of Roman Catholic scholars. No doubt the most comprehensive expositions, the most penetrating analyses, and even the most interesting evaluations of the Church Dogmatics and of the rest of my work have thus far come from the Catholic camp (with the important exceptions of the work of G. C. Berkouwer and that of a young American whose Heidelberg dissertation was recently made accessible to me.) Outstanding among the Catholic studies is the well-known book of my Basel friend Hans Urs von Balthasar. And strange as it may seem in this book the points on which Balthasar and I agree counterbalance those on which we differ. A most extraordinary development is the fact that a young man from Lucerne, for seven years thoroughly trained in Rome and having become a doctor of theology in Paris, has presented in a book razor-sharp arguments for the thesis

that between the Reformation teaching as now interpreted
and presented by myself and the rightly understood doctrine of the Roman Catholic Church there is precisely on
the central point of justification by grace no essential
difference! So far his book has not been repudiated by
Catholic officialdom, but to the contrary has been openly
lauded by various prominent representatives of that
church. What is one to say to that? Has the millennium
broken in, or is it waiting around the next corner? How
one would like to believe it!"[9]

After pointing out factors that may indicate that the
Catholic Church was still not determined by its theological vanguard, Barth added: "It remains an established
fact, however, that such a forward-looking group is at
work - thus far without proscription - and before us,
before me especially, lies the attractive possibility, or
rather necessity, of remaining in touch with this vanguard."[10]

(2) THE CONDITIONS OF A DEMANDING PARTNERSHIP

Let us return now to our first question. Why should
Catholicism to a greater extent than Protestantism be so
obviously interested in seeing anything at all in Barth's
theology? Why did Roman Catholics find in Karl Barth a
fitting, and more than that, an exceptionally admired
and respected partner? We would be tempted to answer
flatly: because he was a real theologian, a great, a
very great theologian, but we have been told that it is
not right for us to declare Barth a great theologian, or
the theologian who was most faithful to God's word.[11]
This kind of sin has, however, been committed time and
again, both by Protestants and Catholics. In the title
of an article of <u>Encounter</u>, Karl Barth has been labeled
"the last great Protestant", and recently a Catholic
writer has called him "a master theologian, the greatest
since Saint Thomas and the only true theologian that
Protestantism ever had". I beg your pardon for repeat-
ing this but I retain that Karl Barth has been accepted
as a partner because he was considered a great theologian,
and not just a great Protestant theologian, a great
Christian theologian, and the greatest of our times.
Balthasar explains that Roman Catholics have learned to
know in Karl Barth a form of Protestantism which has
attained to a genuine Christian Universalism.[12]

BARTH'S IMPACT ON THE CATHOLIC CHURCH

You could legitimately suspect Catholic theologians of some haughtiness if they would give to understand that they could accept dialogue only with some kind of unparalleled genius. The fact is that they found in Barth a unique combination of many factors which rendered the encounter possible, attractive and profitable.

The Jesuit Jean Daniélou, now Cardinal Daniélou, really expressed common Catholic reaction when, in the aftermath of Amsterdam, he wrote: "We have loved Karl Barth very much. We are very thankful to him. This is what we have always said and say again. He has rediscovered the authentic value of the Bible. We have loved Karl Barth as the one who has overcome the dogmatic liberalism for which we have not more consideration than he has. And we have loved his tragic perception of the responsibility of the preacher. If we say no to him today, it is with the sorrow of a great disappointed hope."[13]

For Catholics, the greatness of Barth is again, according to Etienne Gilson in a letter written in 1946, "to have affirmed and maintained for our time the unconditional respect of the Word of God," and to "give back to theology its place and its true essence", to "witness so greatly to the vitality of Christianity."[14] We have heard a general answer to our question: Why did Catholics find a partner in Karl Barth? But we have now to explore the matter in more detail. May I first eliminate one factor that I don't consider decisive for most of the period under study. Though Barth has regularly been hailed as a prophet, I submit that the social, political, and even pastoral dimension of his theology which has today so much appeal, have been taken into account rather late.[15] It has not been primarily because of his anxious concerns as a preacher of the Word, nor because of his stand over against the Nazis, that Karl Barth made an impact on the Catholic Church. It is definitely because of his dogmatic theology, as the Barth of the Römerbrief and the author of Church Dogmatics. But once more, let us further ask why?

Catholics have often underlined that Barth's theology represents an enormous step forward as compared to liberalism. An Italian commentator goes so far as to write that: "the interest it has even for Catholics, consists exclusively in its unyielding opposition to liberal Protestantism and modernism, in the reaffirmation of the transcendence of God and of the absolute gratuity of

Grace".[16] The very fact that Barth had forced Harnack to react could only make him congenial for Catholics. But it is certainly not just for this negative reason - Catholics could have found among their own ranks anti-liberals enough - that they became interested in Barth.

A positive factor could be that they found him acquainted with the whole Catholic heritage. As Balthasar noted, "for Karl Barth the history of the Church of Jesus does not begin with the Reformation but with Jesus."[17] For Barth Church Fathers and Medieval theologians were witnesses to the understanding of Scripture and for him the pronouncements of the early Councils were to be taken seriously. A common acceptance of a long tradition has therefore united Barth and the Catholics against pure biblicists. Still in Balthasar's words: "Thus, in Barth's Dogmatics we find a theology that is coextensive with ours in history and subject matter."[18]

If it was not enough to be anti-liberal, it was not enough either to be somewhat Catholic for Barth's theology to be important to the Catholic Church. If his achievement occasioned such a response, it is rather for a two-fold reason, according to a statement of Balthasar that has been often repeated: "Barth's work, then, has two features. It is the most thorough and forceful systematization of Protestant thought; and it is the closest approximation to Catholic thought".[19]

Let us take for granted - in spite of some strong affirmations to the contrary - that Karl Barth is genuinely Protestant. According to Balthasar "in his work authentic Protestantism has found its full-blown image for the first time."[20] The problem is really in conciliating this fact with the affirmation that Barth was close to Catholic thinking in spite of his imprecations against the analogy of being, of his stand in regard to philosophy and natural theology, or his frequent polemical anticatholic overtone. While one may speak of "an abyss"[21] between Barth and Catholic doctrine, others, like Edward O'Connor, express more correctly the feeling of most Catholics, when he writes: "Even a Catholic, aware that his own position is probably the chief object of Barth's scorn, can nonetheless sense an accord between Barth's position and certain obscure but profound convictions of his own".[22]

We will see later on how substantial agreement has been claimed on such unexpected grounds as analogy, ecclesiology, and justification. Hans Küng has found that Barth's doctrine on grace is reconcilable with Trent, Fries, that his basic ecclesiology does not warrant a church separation, and Chavannes that his doctrine on analogy is not that far from Saint Thomas. Over and above all agreements on particular points, there exists a common concept of theology. Both Barth and the best scholastic tradition represented by Saint Thomas see theology as a function of the Church, both consider theology essentially within the realm of faith. The very first section of the Church Dogmatics on "Dogmatik als Glaubensakt" is witness to that. We may even say that both also understand theology as a rational pursuit, and Barth has been seen by Catholics as offering a third possibility for modern Protestantism often trapped, to their mind, in a dilemma between religiosity devoid of intelligence and intellectualism devoid of faith.[23] It has even been suggested that if Barth has been criticized for his Catholic tendencies, it is mainly because he wanted to present Christian doctrine rationally and propositionally.[24]

Theology however does not exist for its own sake. Why do Catholics find interest and profit in Barth's theology? An ever recurring answer is that it is because he is the champion of God, of the absolute transcendence of God. At a time of persistent and growing sympathy for immanence and for an anthropological approach, Barth's opposition to all those who, in the line of liberalism, seem to place God in the dependence of man, deserved, for many, unconditional admiration and gratitude.[25]

A few Catholics may have misunderstood the nature of the agreement between Barth and their Church. I don't think that very many have nurtured for long the hope that, like Eric Peterson, Barth would sooner or later join the Roman fold. The agreement nonetheless gave after all some weight to people who assumed that Barth, Roman Catholicism, and the Ecumenical Christianity as a whole were all part of the same diabolical plot.

I do not stop at the Reformation Review, though the phenomenon it represents should not be underestimated by the sociologist or the historian of Christianity, even if it fails to be taken in earnest by theologians. Cornelius van Til, with many credentials, arrives at similar conclusions: Karl Barth, Roman Catholicism and Neo-Protestantism replace the Christ of Luther and Calvin with a Christ "patterned after modern activist thought",[26] their theology is informed "by dialectical principles

BARTH'S IMPACT ON THE CATHOLIC CHURCH

that spring from the assumption of human autonomy."[27]
For him Catholic theologians - he discusses at length
Balthasar and Küng - have found a friend in Barth as over
against Luther and Calvin.

(3) THE MEANDERS OF THE DIALOGUE

Looking for the reasons why Karl Barth has become the
partner of Roman Catholicism we have already partly explained how this partnership was established and this
impact made. We must notice that these events happened
in spite of apparently quite inauspicious conditions.
We know how Barth identified Roman Catholicism with the
rationalistic and pietistic trends in part of modern
Protestantism, and how he fought both with equal vigour.
An Anglican writer notes that he suffered "from an incredibly ill-considered bias against Roman Catholicism,
which rarely coincides with the greatness of his own
thought".[28] Avery Dulles puts the problem more nicely:
"An ambivalent love-hate relationship with Rome runs like
an Ariadne's thread through his entire career".[29]

I will not dwell here upon the attacks of Barth against
Catholicism and in particular upon his Amsterdam address
(1948) which deeply hurt Catholic feelings and caused
quite a commotion in the Ecumenical world. In a familiar
talk to members of the Reformed and Presbyterian churches
at Amsterdam, he further uttered the following remarks
which may be the most bitter expression of his attitude
during this period: "Do you agree as members of the Reformed Churches to make yours what I was saying to my
Anglo-Catholic friend Ramsay: I am sorry that you do not
detest the pope? I hope that we are not disappointed because a cardinal sent by the Vatican has not come to sit
at the presidential table with Mr. Boegner. Let us not
be sentimental. We cannot associate with the Roman Church.
Things being what they are, the Catholic Church could not
take towards Amsterdam an attitude different from the one
it took. I thus suggest that you renounce the useless
tears that some are tempted to shed because of the absence
of Rome. Where one says not only Jesus, but Jesus and
Mary, where an earthly authority is acknowledged as infallible, we can only say a resolute No. Our only attitude towards Catholicism is mission or evangelization,
not union. Those who know Calvin should agree with me on
this and not hold that it is a Barthian Fancy."[30]

BARTH'S IMPACT ON THE CATHOLIC CHURCH

Despite admonitions by dear friends of both camps, Barth gave no immediate signs of repentance. It is reported in his Table Talks that he still said much later: "Roman Catholicism is a terrible thing, because it means the imprisonment of God Himself! It claims to be the possessor of the Holy Spirit and revelation and Jesus Christ Himself. Can there be anything more terrible than the identification of God and man! This is worse than any pantheism! It is the more terrible because it is so pious, so beautiful".[31]

For the consolation of Catholics he added that modern Protestantism was as a matter of fact still worse, Roman Catholicism being at least "impressive and interesting". It is this man who practised no sentimental ecumenism, with whom Roman Catholics thought possible a dialogue that could be "healthy and loyal because clear and sincere".[32] Adolf Keller, writing in 1931 about Dialectic Theology in general, affirms that with Barth (and what was still then called Barthianism), the conflict between Roman Catholicism and Protestantism had entered into a new phase. After the inquisition, the anathema and the practical competition, it has supposedly entered the phase of mutual questioning.[33]

Soon after the publication of the Römerbrief, Barth discovered indeed that his thinking had met with an unexpected consideration on the part of Catholic theologians and it seems that he considered this at the time a mixed blessing. He wrote to his friend Eduard Thurneysen on the 5 of February, 1924: "What shall we say of the three Catholic reviews I received recently, of which each one shows still more understanding than the last? Are these people obeying the secret orders of some hidden Roman propaganda office, which already is speculating on our surrender, or are they the voices of the true Una Sancta we ought to be glad to hear? In any case: we should never stick to a too narrow Protestant perspective."[34]

For the two following decades, the names of Przywara, Guardini, Adam, Grosche, Volk, Fehr, Ries, etc. represent important landmarks. I do not think with Keller, that Roman Catholics have been moved directly to establish a common front in the struggle against secularism and other ideologies.[35] But though denouncing what they consider the onesidedness of Barth in his theology of God and Grace, they acknowledged that a common theological thought was possible. Already for this period prevailed the attitude defined later on by Hans Küng: "This is not a business of being for Barth or against Barth. What matters is the indivisible truth of Jesus Christ ... Again, we wish neither to write Barth off as a heretic nor to list him as a crypto-Catholic among our hitherto hidden assets. In this sense the issue is not Barth at all - and he would be the first to agree - but the confronting of one another with the mirror of the gospel of Jesus Christ, in earnest and uncompromising theological interchange."[36]

We must inquire how this new possibility evolved. It is really only after the War, when more favourable conditions prevailed, and after the publication of the Church Dogmatics progressed, that major works began to appear on Barth, and that different trends became manifest. It is not for me to decide who have been objectively the best interpreters of Barth and I can do no more now, than to point out a few great moments and a few important participants in the confrontation between Barth and Catholic theologians. If we were to select one author and one book for their significance in this regard we would have to go back to the decisive contribution of the Swiss Hans Urs von Balthasar: Karl Barth. Darstellung und Deutung seiner Theologie, published in 1951.[37] Barth himself often referred to his shrewd friend from the other side. Balthasar has seldom made the headlines, he is no popular theologian, he took as far as I know no direct part in Vatican II, but he is one of the last humanists in the great Catholic tradition, an original thinker, a brilliant writer, an artist. He was the kind of man who could understand Barth and be understood by him.

The main intent of Balthasar's book which helped so much in making Barth's theology a lively issue in the Catholic Church was to show that about God, creation, christology and atonement, Barth was in substantial agreement with Catholic doctrines. Balthasar clearly explained his initial purpose for the English edition last year: "We have examined Barth's outlook on nature and grace and then offered a Catholic Christocentric viewpoint on the same topic. In so doing, we observed a gradual rapprochement taking place. This does not mean that both sides are in full agreement, nor need they be....

"My book, then, has achieved its purpose. It has shown

that the problems and approaches of Barth are not such
that they justify or necessitate a split in the Church.
Here, of course, I am only talking about the problems
raised in the tracts on God as creator, sanctifier, and
redeemer (<u>de Deo creante</u>, <u>elevante</u>, <u>redimente</u>) not about
the tracts on the Church and the sacraments."[38]

In the meantime French speaking theologians had also
begun to offer their contribution. The first book was
authored by the Dominican Jérôme Hamer, presently on the
Roman Secretariate for Unity. Though probably overly
critical, it was a valuable pioneer attempt at discerning Barth's method and approach. Hamer summed up his
main concern in his original title: "<u>L'occasionalisme
théologique de Karl Barth</u>" which was not retained for
the English translation.[39] It has been claimed that
Hamer was imposing on Barth a straightjacket, transforming a flexible and ever developing theology into a rigid
system.[40] Hamer indirectly answered his critics in the
forward to the English translation, while retaining his
basic reservations. These reservations he worded elsewhere strongly: "The great general weakness of Barth's
theology, even in its most recent expressions, resides
in the lack of consistency it gives to anything that is
human."[41]

A few years later the Jesuit Henri Bouillard offered
us a three volume work which remains to this date the
most comprehensive introduction to Barth and his best
critique, though it still concentrates on the main doctrines connected with God's interpellation and Man's
response.[42] Bouillard had on June 16, 1956, the redoubtable honour of defending his dissertation before the
grand jury of the Sorbonne, in the presence of Barth,
reduced to silence by an inflexible protocol.

Bouillard spells out his purpose: "In taking up the
basic problems which are today, as before, the meetingground for the exchange between nature and grace, we
have thought it well to do this in the form of a dialogue
with Karl Barth. There are two advantages to this procedure. On the one hand, the radical position adopted by
Barth demands radical reflection on our part. On the
other hand, because Barth deals in his work with the
whole of the Christian tradition and defines his positions with regard to a number of theologians and philosophers, he affords us the opportunity to envisage the
same problems from various perspectives."[43]

BARTH'S IMPACT ON THE CATHOLIC CHURCH

"If we cannot escape debate, we shall not, however, make of it the principal object of our efforts. The angle under which we have chosen to study Barthian thought has led us to neglect (or very nearly) those questions with reference to which the differences between Catholics, and Protestants are most obvious: the structure of the Church, the relation between Scripture and tradition, the understanding of the sacraments, Marian doctrine, etc. Our attention will be occupied with questions of a wider nature which are, generally speaking, situated on the frontiers between theology and philosophy."[44]

Balthasar approves of Foley's characterization of Bouillard's book: "Bouillard has probed deeper into the nooks and corners of Barth's thought, and he has subjected Barth's theology to a thoroughgoing critique. In so doing, he has introduced elements from the theology of Rudolf Bultmann. In the last analysis, however, Bouillard and I are admittedly in agreement on the basic positions concerning fundamental theology."[45]

To hear that Balthasar agrees with Bouillard may be a surprise. As a matter of fact Bouillard probably holds a middle position between the more severe and the more lenient critics. It is the latter who were soon to receive new and strong support.

Just as Balthasar had concluded that the series of problems he had examined were no ground for a split in the Church, a well-known German theologian Heinrich Fries, the predecessor of Küng at Tübingen, brought forth a similar proposition about Barth's basic idea of the Church (excluding of course the particular problems of Church structures, ministry and sacraments).[46] Even the British Hugo Meynell came along the same line at the end of a rather critical essay.[47]

The most influential book for its wide impact on the whole ecumenical scene is Hans Küng's Paris dissertation on justification.[48] It is too well known for me to dwell on its content. Be it sufficient to recall its startling thesis. Within the scope of the question of justification and related problems, Barth has again no genuine argument for separation from the ancient church, or at least an interpretation compatible with Catholic orthodoxy.

The argument was strengthened by Barth writing the author that his position had fully and accurately been reproduced. Consequently, if what is presented by Küng as Catholic doctrine is really the teaching of his Church, then Barth admits that his own view of justification agrees with the Catholic views.

Küng's book has probably elicited more response than any other comparable theological work. In this manner, at least, Karl Barth was having a universal impact on the Catholic world. Nobody writing on the subject of grace and justification could now afford to ignore Küng and Barth. Theologians of all schools in Germany, in France, in Switzerland, in Belgium, in the Netherlands, in Rome, took sides, most agreeing substantially that Küng had not only correctly interpreted Barth, but that he also had correctly interpreted the Council of Trent.[49] Hans Küng could write in 1964, for the English translation of his book: "The discussion to date has not brought forth irreducible distinctions between the Barthian and the Catholic doctrines of justification which would divide the Church and not just a school."[50]

Balthasar underlined that the focal concern of Küng provides an even more determined profile of the Christocentric emphasis which he propounded as the proper plane for dialogue.[51]

Another breakthrough seems to have happened most recently. Henri Chavannes, in a book unlikely to arouse now as much passion, has conducted a thorough comparison between Karl Barth and Saint Thomas on the disputed question of the analogy between God and the world. We know that the <u>analogia entis</u> has been for a time the chief heresy opposed by Barth who seems to have confused the personal speculations of Przywara with the genuine thomistic notion of analogy.[52]

As we have seen, although several Catholic theologians have been laudatory and have endeavoured to find approximations with Barth, most have also formulated fundamental criticisms. They have, on the whole, been strongly against the so-called dialectic theology and have mellowed in the measure where they have perceived a real evolution in Barth's thinking as expressed in the <u>Church Dogmatics</u>. Hamer, together with the Dutch J.C. Groot[53] have underlined forcefully basic objections to the Barthian system. For Hamer this system is essentially based upon the actual and discontinued character of the Word of God and on its essentially mysterious character, which leads to the <u>Credo quia absurdum</u> and leaves an irremediable gap between two levels, action of God and action of man.[54]

BARTH'S IMPACT ON THE CATHOLIC CHURCH

Henri Bouillard was just as strong about the dialectic period: "God is so totally the unique author of our relation with him that this relation exists only where he limits us, denies us, suppresses us."[55] Karl Barth is seen as more radical than the Reformers in his rejection of man's cooperation with God and this would affect his idea of the Incarnation, of justification, of natural theology, of natural law, of self knowledge.[56] For these critics transcendence as understood by Barth implies an absence of communication.

Avery Dulles has singled out some consequences of this general attitude: Karl Barth was too radical in his repudiation of culture-Christianity, too narrow in his evaluation of other religions, he did not take the historical problem seriously enough, he disparaged the demands of autonomous reason.[57] Yves Congar, a French dominican who has been particularly influential in the context of Vatican II, has also expressed the same very strong reservations about Barth: "While liberating Protestantism from humanistic rationalism, he has renewed and reinforced in it a ferment of heresy the results of which are disastrous. I mean this tendency to consider the sovereign causality of God in God alone, without seeing what reality this causality places in us."[58]

Several watched closely for a further evolution in Barth's thinking. Some found in the 1956 lecture published under the title The Humanity of God the signs of a turning point in his theology.[59] It finally appeared that if there was an evolution still in progress there was no break with the past. Nonetheless the overall image of the relationship of Barth with Roman Catholicism remains that of a positive and mutually enriching dialogue which was dramatically highlighted by Barth's visit to Rome in September 1966.

As far back as 1928, Barth had been aware that in the lower regions of inter-confessional polemics, some of his remarks could be used as arguments for Roman Catholicism. But he had not taken this prospect as an excuse to by-pass the real questions of the Catholic Church.[60]

From the beginning Barth had been concerned with Vatican II and, at the request of Dr. Visser't Hooft, had expressed his thoughts on the Council.[61] On account of his poor health, he had been later unable to accept an invitation to be an observer. But after the celebration of his 80th birthday he temporarily gave up work on his autobiography to make, in his own words, his peregrinatio ad limina apostolorum, his pilgrimage to the threshold of the apostles. He wanted to obtain first hand information on how the decisions of the Council were understood in Rome, so he took with him a list of 79 questions which he presented to a series of academic or ecclesiastical authorities. He even asked the pope if in the phrase "fratres sejuncti" (separated brethren) one was to emphasize the brethren or the separated.[62]

Let me quote excerpts from his description of an event I had personally the privilege to witness: "On the final day of our stay we had the opportunity to participate in the International Congress of Theologians who were then gathered in Rome from all parts of the globe. In the lobby of the meeting hall we were surprised by a united choir of young Protestants and Catholics from Wettingen in Aargau, who welcomed us there in the center of Rome with Nr. 73 from our hymnal...I was greeted by applause, honored by a respectful greeting, personally introduced together with the cardinals who were present... We heard a lecture by Karl Rahner on the presence of Jesus Christ in the Eucharist, in which only the frequent use of the modern word existentialis sounded rather queer to me, and a discussion led by Professor Semmelroth."[63]

No doubt Barth has been given in Rome a treatment that would not have been granted to any other scholar from within or from outside the Catholic Church. This is in some way a measure of the impact he had made. In one of his very last statements Barth still mentioned that he was in very good terms with many Catholic theologians, at times in better terms than with Protestants.[64] There was now a sense of belonging together which did not exclude deep searching, but which went farther than just speaking at one another and even than mutual questioning.

(4) THE MEASURE OF A PERVADING INFLUENCE

How to evaluate the influence of Barth or the effects of his impact? It would be easy to form a collection of general remarks like: "Certainly his influence upon several outstanding Catholic theologians is well known";[65] or: "The influence of Barth on Roman Catholic world is great";[66] or: "The influence of that breakthrough has reached beyond Protestantism into the Roman Church and

BARTH'S IMPACT ON THE CATHOLIC CHURCH

bears at least some responsibility for the reformation which it has been experiencing in recent years";[67] or: "The pinch of spice that Barth has called his theology has already considerably seasoned Catholic thought through Roman Catholic commentators and students."[68] It has even been suggested that Barth's impact has been more evident in Roman Catholicism than in much of the Protestant world.[69]

The major question, of course, is whether Barth has had a significant influence on the Council and its preparation? Avery Dulles answers: "The change in Barth's attitude toward the Catholic Church should be attributed not so much to his own mellowing (though he did mellow) as to the inner transformation of Catholic theology itself in the 1940's and 1950's, partly under the influence of Protestants such as himself. For alert Catholic thinkers on the European continent, the dialogue with neo-orthodoxy stimulated many new insights. Authors such as de Lubac, Congar, Danielou, Bouillard, Bouyer, Rahner and Balthasar took very seriously the Barthian critique of Catholicism. Moving away from the Scholastic and juridical emphasis of post-Tridentine Catholicism, they forged within the Catholic tradition a theology that aimed to be authentically evangelical, kerygmatic and christocentric."[70]

Karl Barth has undoubtedly helped many Roman Catholics to rediscover part of their own authentic tradition. An Irish theologian Colm O'Grady even feels that Catholics have already listened to the basic positive demands of Karl Barth: "Barth has contributed enormously to the recent renewal in Catholic theology, and especially in its theology of the Church. He epitomizes in fact many of the advances made by Vatican II. Its primary emphasis on Jesus Christ and the Holy Spirit in relation to the Church, its dynamic and joyful presentation of Christian life, etc., were already his."[71]

If Barth directly influenced Catholic theology, his impact on the Catholic Church was also indirect but powerful through the ecumenical movement. Barth was no ecumenical theologian in the ordinary meaning of the word, but according to Willems: "When theology really immerses itself in the mystery of God's revelation and in so doing invites co-thinking and co-meditating in the whole of the area of the faith, then it is both Kerygmatic and ecumenical."[72]

BARTH'S IMPACT ON THE CATHOLIC CHURCH

In spite of all these affirmations one could yet play the devil's advocate and question the influence of Barth as did one writer in 1966: "Still it is true that for many Catholic theologians, the great majority of priests and most educated Catholic laymen, the name of Barth means very little, and the name of Bultmann even less. This, of course, is even more acutely true in America than in Europe."[73]

If I try to recall the 50's, when I was a student of theology, first in Ottawa and then in Innsbruck, I would be tempted to say that Karl Barth was indeed a big name, but that he had little direct influence, although I would not dare to say that he did not have, even then, some diffused impact.

An adequate survey should cover at least courses given in universities, and seminaries, dissertations and publications, and this will probably never be done. For the sake of curiosity I have looked in the name index of a few collective works describing the contemporary situation. The two big tomes published in 1957 by the theological faculty of Milan, with the collaboration of a wide range of authorities, give an excellent idea of preconciliar theology. In the index Barth appears among the authors most referred to, after only Augustine, Thomas Aquinas and the now already forgotten Dominican Garigou-Lagrange, those following closely being Pius XII, Congar, Malevez and Michel.[74]

Fragen der Theologie Heute, published the same year, a similar though less audacious enterprise conducted by Swiss theologians and practically restricted to German speaking collaborators, gives a clear lead to Karl Rahner and Karl Barth, in the distinguished company of Augustine, Bultmann, Congar, Cullmann, Luther, Pius XII, and Thomas Aquinas.[75] A recent Bilan de la theologie de XXe siecle, a joint project of French and German speaking scholars, gives Karl Rahner the first rank, followed almost immediately by Barth, Bultmann and Thomas Aquinas, and then by Augustine, von Balthasar, Congar, Heidegger, De Lubac, Schillebeeckx.[76]

The influence of Barth in the German language area, or even in the Netherlands, is almost taken for granted. I have therefore endeavoured to give preferential attention to those sections of the Catholic world less likely to have experienced the impact of Barth.

Thanks mainly to the Dominican G. Rabeau and the Jesuit

BARTH'S IMPACT ON THE CATHOLIC CHURCH

L. Malevez who quite regularly wrote review articles, French speaking theologians began as soon as the late 20's and the early 30's to become aware of the importance of Barth. Early reports may betray an unconscious mistrust of Protestant theology but they also give way to the intuition that something new was happening within Christianity.[77] In 1934 Yves Congar invited Karl Barth for a colloquium in which took part Gilson, Maritain, Gabriel Marcel, Pierre Maury. He himself offered at that time at the Dominican Faculty of Le Saulchoir, a course on the theology of Barth.[78]

While the influence of Barth was declining in Protestant Germany after World War II, the interest in him was rather increasing in France and Switzerland among the French speaking Reformed. Writing a preface for the original edition of his book, in 1949, Jérôme Hamer could nevertheless still write: "Practically unknown in France until 1933, today his thought distinctly characterizes a group of Protestant thinkers of ever-increasing importance. In some measure he even attracts the attention of Catholic thinkers. And yet, no one familiar with dialectical theology can fail to notice the superficiality of the information on a subject that arouses such keen interest. Diametrically opposed theories are blandly combined under Karl Barth's name."[79]

The three volume work of Bouillard mentioned before probably encompasses more of Barth-thinking than any other work in any language, and has proved too much of a challenge for translators. Bouillard thus made Karl Barth really available to the French public who had never been perfectly at ease with the complexity and abundance of Barth's writing.[80]

Thanks to the Waldensians, Italy was also early enough made acquainted with Barth. The first notable Catholic contribution is the Book of Emmanuelle Riverso which Barth has listed among the best on his theology. Riverso felt it necessary to state that "only in Catholicism, can the vital exigencies of Barthianism have an exact signification and a true efficacy."[81] Another Italian, B. Gherardini has written several essays on Barth and has even at times defended him against those who believed in the persistence of his actualism.[82]

Spanish language areas had been introduced to Barth by Ortega y Gasset and Unamuno. Understanding for Barth's teaching among Spanish theologians went deeper than one expected and Barth, during his trip to Rome, alludes with praise to the Jesuit Alfaro.[83] Even Portugal eventually heard the good news.[84]

The first significant Catholic study I know in English is from Hugo Meynell, lecturer at the University of Leeds when his book was published. He examined the questions of natural theology, creation, Jesus Christ and human existence, and objected that Barth's emphasis on the absolute sovereignty of God was at the price of human existence though his general conclusion sounded more optimistic.[85]

A more ambitious undertaking from the British Isles is the study of Colm O'Grady on the ecclesiology of Karl Barth and on the Catholic ecclesiology in dialogue with Karl Barth, first presented as a dissertation at the Gregorian University in Rome and published in two volumes in 1968 and 1969. O'Grady aims at a better Catholic understanding of Protestantism, at an illustration of the actual ecclesiological agreements between Barth and the Catholic Church, and finally at a real dialogue. Accordingly to him the average pre-conciliar Catholic treatise would have very much to learn from Karl Barth, and he tries himself to develop Catholic ecclesiology along the line suggested by him, that is, with an emphasis on the spiritual, christological and Trinitarian aspects.[86]

If we cross the Atlantic we must acknowledge a void which has but very lately begun to be filled. When Arnold S. Nash in his introduction to the <u>Protestant Thought in the Twentieth Century</u> speaks of the supremacy of American influence even in religious matters, it certainly does not apply to our particular field of research.[87] "The American resistance to Barth", the phrase is from Robert McAfee Brown,[88] is an accepted fact for American Protestantism and it is just more true for Catholic theologians. Such a distinguished scholar as the late G. Weigel seemed still to retain, in 1950, a rather negative and, I would even say, primitive view of Barth. Referring to his lectures on the Creed, Weigel makes these surprising comments: "In the light of these observations on the Barthian work it need hardly be said that a Catholic gains no great satisfaction on reading Barth's seemingly orthodox explanation of the articles of the Apostles' Creed. He believes in God, the God of the Bible. He believes that God is one in three persons, though he tells us that this only means that God exists and acts in three ways. Is this fourth century modalism

BARTH'S IMPACT ON THE CATHOLIC CHURCH

come back to life? Barth insists energetically on the divinity of Jesus Christ, according to the Nicene Creed. He believes in the reality and divinity of the Holy Spirit. Yet all these affirmations - and their sincerity cannot be doubted in the slightest - have as much value as the meanings attached to the words. But such meanings will be expressed by concepts, and toward concepts Barth is rather cavalier."[89]

Weigel affirms that no enthusiasm is engendered in him by the Barthian orthodoxy, for he does not know whether Barth and himself have met the same Christ, but he is rather moved by Barth's singular charm in presenting many Christian dogmas, and by his warmth and rich appreciation of some of their obscurer facets.

Essays collected in 1968 by James F. Andres, then managing editor of the National Catholic Reporter,[90] include only, in reference to the Catholic scene, together with extracts of Küng's book on justification, an appraisal by Edward D. O'Connor of Karl Barth's visit in Chicago, characteristic enough of American Catholics' uncertainty about Barth. Another symptom of the belated interest of English speaking Catholics for Barth is the fact that several of the most significant books on him have been translated only after a number of years, twelve years for H. Fries and even much more in the case of von Balthasar's book about which a reviewer writes that "the mystery question to ask American publishers is why we had to wait 20 years for an English version of this classic evaluation of Barthian thought."[91]

What should we conclude from this necessarily superficial and inadequate survey? That Karl Barth has been so widely read and so constantly submitted to benevolent or rigorous criticism, already implies that he had quite an impact on the Catholic Church. It does not necessarily imply however, that he has had a direct influence, since he could have been studied for the mere sake of knowledge, or just to be more effectively opposed, but this was hardly the case.

Barth's theology has been a wonderful challenge to Catholic theologians. He has forced them to revise their traditional positions, he has made it impossible for them to indulge in the false security of simple repetition. His imprecations have brought them to emphasize or, on the contrary, to pedal down different aspects of their theology. Even the acknowledgement of an approximation with him does not exclude the possibility of some subtle influence. Barth astutely asked Hans Küng what he could have asked Balthasar, Fries, and many others: "May I just whisper a question (a very confidential question..): Did you yourself discover all this before you so carefully read my <u>Church Dogmatics</u> or was it while you were reading it or afterward?"92 The least we can say is that no close intellectual contact can exist without some form of influence and as Fransen writes about Küng's book, Barth's theology has at least the immense advantage of reminding Catholics that "there are more things in heaven and earth than are dreamed of in our ... theology".93

While a number of individual Catholic theologians could have joined Küng in his personal tribute at the burial, or could speak warmly with Bouillard of their personal gratitude towards Barth,94 I assume that many more could not very well define their relationship with him. I assume that Catholics could produce comments not very different from those collected fifteen years ago in <u>Theology Today</u>.95 For some, the influence of Karl Barth has been chiefly indirect. He has helped give courage. For many he is the man who has proclaimed the need of returning to the main Christian assumptions (though for Protestants it may mean recover the fundamentals, and for Catholics discard some accidentals), he has been the prophet of God's otherness, of the Christological concentration, of the uniqueness of Biblical Revelation, of faith. He has marked a shift of emphasis from man to God.

CONCLUSION

I assume that most of us do not claim to be prophets nor seers. We can nevertheless inquire, even if with modesty, about the future. As I understand it, a Society for the study of Karl Barth is established, it is anticipated that his theology has a future of some kind. To be honest, at the time of Karl Barth's death, and ever since, this future has appeared grim to many. A. Dulles spoke of the "post Barthian phase".96 J.C. Bennett admitted that Barth was now virtually ignored in the theological discussion and that even in Europe he had ceased to be the towering figure he was.97 Ironically, the obituary of the Catholic Commonweal was written by Harvey Cox who observed that most of Barth's thoughts were swimming against the present current.98 At least two

BARTH'S IMPACT ON THE CATHOLIC CHURCH

Roman Catholics have suggested that the answer given by Barth to Schleiermacher should not be considered definitive.[99]

It has been recently questioned by a French theologian whether such an admirable (and probably enduring) form of theology as represented by Barth and his friend Balthasar, could not in fact precipitate the divorce between faith and reason. God and the World, Church and history.[100] This is indeed a concern which does not seem to have bothered Barth, but which keeps bothering many within and outside the Catholic tradition.

Balthasar has affirmed that "Barth will never be out of date for us Catholics so long as we have not confronted his ideas and found answers for the question he asks."[101] At the end of the Council it consequently appeared that the dialogue between Barth and the Roman Catholic Church would be crucial for the future. It is doubtful now that these problems will occupy the mind of the theologians as they did in the past. Re-thinking doctrine along more biblical lines, as does for example Hans Küng for ecclesiology, may not be the main theological occupation of tomorrow. Even today Catholic theologians respond as much to Bultmann, Bonhoeffer or Pannenberg as to Barth. But who can tell what it will be tomorrow?

Barth once asked the embarrassing question: "Is it so certain that dialogue with the world is to be placed ahead of proclamation to the world?"[102] We can only say, that the trend which finds its voice in the Dogmatic constitution on the Word of God apparently did not take precedence in the last years over the one manifested by the Pastoral constitution on the Church and the World. As a matter of fact Karl Barth has been worried by recent developments of Catholic theology. Among his questions about the Council, there was one directly aimed at the progressists: "Are the adherents of the progressive majority of the Council...aware of the danger that this /a renewal in the light of the modern world/ might result in an undesired repetition of the errors committed in modern Protestantism?"[103] About the trends existing since the Council he also wrote: "In looking at it we can only wish that we had something comparable, if it could avoid a repetition of at least the worst mistakes we have made since the sixteenth century."[104]

Barth was aware that his questioning could well be used within the Catholic Church to halt some of the progressive forces at work. When the editor of the Theologisch praktische Quartalschrift asked him to explain his statement on the progressive Catholics he, on second thought, refrained from it on the ground that it would do no good. He had long made himself clear enough on this point and he was glad with adding these noble words: "I would not like however in the present circumstances to enter as the accusor of my brothers, neither the new-Protestants nor the progressive Catholics."105

A Portuguese eulogist of Barth wrote that there are two categories of geniuses: geniuses of the dawn and geniuses of the twilight: genios da aurora and genios do entardecer, that is geniuses who initiate movements like Plato, Descartes, Einstein, and geniuses who rather sum up or top a period, like Aristotle, Thomas Aquinas, Dante, Hegel.106 The same question has been put about Augustine that we may now put about Barth. Is he for the Christian World in general and the Roman Church in particular, the symbol of a vanishing universe, or is he pointing at a new beginning? Avery Dulles wisely comments: "Only history - or perhaps only the eschaton - will tell us whether Barth's was the last gigantic effort of classical Christianity to assert biblical dualism in the face of modern immanentism and evolutionism."107

We can say no more.

NOTES

1 Cf, B.A. Willems Karl Barth: An Ecumenical Approach to his Theology (Glenrock N.J. 1965)
2 H. Bouillard 'Karl Barth et le catholicisme' Revue de Théologie et de philosophie, 20 (1970) pp 353-367
3 G. Foley 'The Catholic Critics of Karl Barth in Outline and Analysis' Scottish Journal of Theology 14 (1961) pp 136-155; Id, 'Das Verhältnis Karl Barths zum Römischen Katholizismus' Parrhesia; Karl Barth zum achtzigsten Geburtstag am 10. Mai 1966 (Zürich 1966) 598-616. See also, among the relevant literature: A. Keller Karl Barth and Christian Unity (London 1933) 207-224; R.B. Hoyle The Teaching of Karl Barth, An Exposition (London 1939) 48-56; G.C. Niftrik Een beroerder Israëls. Enkele hoofdgedachten in de teologie van Karl Barth (2e ed, Nijkerk 1949) 219-257; K.G. Steck 'Ueber das ekklesiologische Gespräch zwischen Karl Barth und Erich Przywara 1927/

29' Antwort: Karl Barth zum siebzigsten Geburstag am 10. Mai 1956 (Zürich 1956) 249-265; B. Neunheuser 'La teologia protestante in Germania' in Problemi e Orientamenti di Teologia dommatica (Milan 1957) vol I 616-629; G. Philips 'Trois ouvrages catholiques sur la theologie de Karl Barth' Ephemerides theologicae lovanienses 34 (1958) 48-55; J. Hamer Karl Barth 'Introduction to the American Edition. A Reflective Glance and Precisions' (London 1962) XI - XXXVIII; E. Lamirande 'Roman Catholic Reactions to Karl Barth's Ecclesiology' Canadian Journal of Theology 14 (1968) 28-42; S. Ruggiero 'La dottrina di K. Barth sulla conoscenza di Dio nella valulazione dei critici' Laurentianum 12 (1971) 65-90, 198-212. Karl Barth has had few contacts with Eastern Christianity. Berdjaev has objected to several aspects of his thought. Cf, Th. Strotmann 'Karl Barth et l'Orient chretien' dans Irenikon 42 (1969) 33-52

4 H. Küng 'Tribute to Karl Barth' Journal of Ecumenical Studies 6 (1969) 233
5 Ibid, 234
6 See, along that line: J. Hoffman 'Karl Barth, un partenaire exigeant' Bible et Vie chrétienne Nr 87 (1969) 62-65
7 G. Casalis, Portrait of Karl Barth (Garden City N. Y. 1964) 3
8 Ibid, 4
9 Karl Barth How I Changed My Mind (Richmond Va. 1966) 69-70
10 Ibid, 70
11 H.M. Rumscheidt 'A Thank you for Karl Barth' Canadian Journal of Theology 15 (1969) 199
12 H. Urs von Balthasar 'Christlicher Universalismus' Antwort 240
13 J. Daniélou, etc, Gespräche nach Amsterdam (Zürich 1949) 4
14 E. Gilson 'Lettre' Hommage et reconnaissance. Recueil de travaux publiés à l'occasion du soixantième anniversaire de Karl Barth (Neuchatel - Paris 1946) 41
15 Cf, however, H. Bouillard Karl Barth vol I 243-262.
16 B. Gherardini La seconda riforma vol II (Brescia 1966) 189
17 H. Urs von Balthasar loc cit
18 Id, The Theology of Karl Barth (New York 1971) 20
19 Ibid

20 Ibid, 19
21 B. Gherardini loc cit
22 E.D. O'Connor 'Karl Barth in Chicago' J.F. Andrews ed, Karl Barth (St. Louis Miss, 1969) 33 (reprinted from The Review of Politics vol 24, 1962)
23 Ibid, 32
24 W. Nicholls Systematic and Philosophical Theology (Middlesex 1959) 146
25 Cf, J. Hamer Karl Barth (London 1962) 290-291; H. Chavannes L'analogie entre Dieu et le monde selon saint Thomas d'Aquin et selon Karl Barth (Paris 1969) 306-307
26 C. Van Til Christianity and Barthianism (Philadelphia 1962) VII
27 Ibid, 319
28 U.T. Homes 'Barth as Ecumenical Theologian' Encounter 28 (1967) 174
29 A. Dulles 'Karl Barth: A Catholic Appreciation' Christian Century 86 (1969) 408
30 K. Barth 'Les Eglises reformées au sein du conseil oecumenique' Foi et Vie 46 (1948) 495
31 J.D. Godsey ed, Karl Barth's Table Talk (Edinburgh 1963) 43
32 P. Fransen 'Hans Küng on Karl Barth' Month 36 (1966) 42
33 A. Keller op cit, 213
34 Gottesdienst - Menschendienst, Festschrift für Eduard Thurneysen zum 70. Geburtstag (Zürich 1958) quoted by P. Fransen, loc cit, 41
35 Cf, A. Keller op cit, 213
36 H. Küng Justification: The Doctrine of Karl Barth and a Catholic Reflection (New York 1964) XXIII - XXIV
37 A second edition was published in 1962. Cf, W. Kreck 'Analogia fidei oder analogia entis'? Antwort 272-286.
38 H. Urs von Balthasar The Theology of Karl Barth 285-286
39 J. Hamer L'occasionalisme théologique de Karl Barth (Paris 1949) Cf, B. Montagnes 'Parole de Dieu et parole humaine' Revue thomiste 52 (1952) 209-215
40 Cf, J.L. Leuba 'Karl Barth systématisé' Verbum Caro 4 (1950) 182-187.
41 J. Hamer 'La foi comme événement et comme signification. A propos de l'oeuvre du P. Henri Bouillard sur Karl Barth' Nouvelle Revue théologique 81 (1959) 377
42 H. Bouillard Karl Barth (Paris 1957) 3 vol

43 Ibid, vol II p 11, after a partial translation in Cross Currents 18 (1968) 204
44 Ibid, 16-17 (Cross Currents 207)
45 H. Urs von Balthasar The Theology of Karl Barth 297-298
46 H. Fries 'Kirche als Ereignis. Zu Karl Barths Lehre von der Kirche', Catholica 11 (1958) 81-107
47 H.V. Meynell Grace versus Nature. Studies in Karl Barth's Church Dogmatics, (London 1965) 281
48 H. Küng Rechtfertigung. Die Lehre Karl Barths und eine katholische Besinnung (Einsiedeln 1957)
49 Cf, B. Willems op cit, 85-92. K. Rahner, among many others, has backed Küng's main contention: 'Zur Theologie der Gnade' Theologische Quartalschrift 138 (1958) 40-78; Schriften zur Theologie vol. IV (Einsieldeln 1960) 237-271. Among reviewers who have been more critical: J. Ratzinger Theologische Revue 54 (1958) 30-35; B.A. Willems 'Christus und die Kirche' Trierer theologische Zeitschrift 67 (1958) 257-273.
50 H. Küng Justification XIII
51 H. Urs von Balthasar op cit, 298
52 H. Chavannes op cit, 9, 14-15, 302, 205; Cf, A. Patfoort 'Vers une reconciliation entre saint Thomas et Karl Barth' Angelicum 48 (1971) 226-232. Much has been written on the topic of analogy. Among the literature mentioned by Chavannes, see: K. Hammer 'Analogia relationis gegen Analogia entis' Parrhesia 288-304 in particular about Przywara, Söhngen and Balthasar.
53 J.C. Groot Karl Barth en het theologische kenprobleem (Heiloo 1946); his exposition of the Catholic position has been found inadequate by L. Malevez 'Een recente confrontatie van de theologie van Karl Barth met de Katholieke theologie' Bijdragen 9 (1948) 59-71. We could perhaps list E. Riverso together with Hamer and Groot
54 J. Hamer op cit, the whole chapter XI
55 H. Bouillard op cit, vol I 26
56 Ibid, vol II-2. L. Bouyer affirmed that Barth was unfaithful both to the Bible and the Reformers: 'Karl Barth vu par le Pere Bouillard' Revue des sciences religieuses 32 (1958) 260-264
57 A. Dulles loc cit, 409-410
58 Y. Congar Chretiens en dialogue (Paris 1964) XXI Cf, Id, Vraie et fausse reforme dans l'Eglise (Paris 1950, 439-447, 479, 502; 'Pour le dialogue avec le

mouvement oecumenique' Verbum Caro 4 (1950) 120
59 Cf, E. Lamirande loc cit, 38-41; G. Thils 'Chronique de theologie protestante et d'oecumenisme', Ephemerides theologicae lovanienses 33 (1957) 511-514; J.N. Walty 'Chronique de theologie protestante', Revue des sciences philosophique et theologique 48 (1964) 133-134; H. Fries loc cit, 81
60 Cf, B. Willems op cit, 77-78
61 K. Barth 'Thoughts on the Second Vatican Council' Ecumenical Review 15 (1963) 357-367
62 Id, Ad Limina Apostolorum. An appraisal of Vatican II (Richmond Va, 1968) 9-18; Cf, H. Bouillard 'Karl Barth et le Catholicisme' loc cit, 361-364; A.J.M. van Weers 'Karl Barth Goes to Rome' Frontier 19 (1967) 91-92; Ch. Journet 'Karl Barth: Ad Limina Apostolorum' Nova et Vetera 43 (1968) 245-273; R. Marlé 'Les questions de Karl Barth relatives à la déclaration conciliare sur la liberte réligieuse'; E. Castelli ed, L'herméneutique et la liberté religieuse (Paris 1968) 411-424
63 K. Barth Ad Limina Apostolorum 13
64 Derniers temoignages (Geneve 1970) 33
65 H.G. Wells 'Karl Barth's Doctrine of Analogy' Canadian Journal of Theology 16 (1970) 213
66 W. Dantine 'Ist Barth überholt?' in W. Dantine and K. Lüthi ed, Theologie zwischen Gestern und Morgen. Interpretationen und Anfragen zum Werk Karl Barths, (München 1968) 39
67 J.D. Smart The Divided Mind of Modern Theology. Karl Barth and Rudolf Bultmann 1908-1933 (Philadelphia 1967) 8
68 C.F. Starkloff The Office of Proclamation in the Theology of Karl Barth (Ottawa 1969) 136. Karl Barth presented his theology as a kind of marginal note (Randbemerkung).
69 'Karl Barth' Christianity Today 13 (1969) 310
70 A. Dulles loc cit, 409
71 C. O'Grady The Church in Catholic Theology: Dialogue with Karl Barth (London 1969); Cf, H. Bouillard 'Karl Barth et le Catholicisme' loc cit, 364-365
72 B. Willems op cit, p 76; cf, pp 82-85. See W.A. Visser 't Hooft, 'Message oecumenique' Les Cahiers du Renouveau Nr 13 (May 1956) 43-43; Id, 'In Memoriam Karl Barth' Oekumenische Rundschau 18 (1969) 248
73 L. Swidler Introduction to H. Fries: Bultmann-Barth and Catholic Theology (Pittsburg 1967) 17

74 Problemi e orientamenti di teologia dommatica 2 vols, (Milan 1957); it is amazing that there is but one reference to Barth in G. Thils, Orientations de la théologie (Louvain 1958)
75 J. Feiner etc, ed, Fragen der Theologie Heute (Zürich-Köln 1957)
76 R. Vander Gucht and H. Vorgrimler ed, Bilan de la théologie du XXe siècle (Tournai 1970); simultaneously published in German by Herder.
77 Cf, L. Malevez 'Un mouvement recent de la théologie protestante. L'école de Karl Barth' Nouvelle Revue Théologique 55 (1928) 650-663; G. Rabeau 'Théologie protestante allemande' Revue des Sciences philosophique et théologique 19 (1930) 359-386
78 Cf, Y. Congar Chrétiens en dialogue XX-XXI
79 J. Hamer Karl Barth V
80 B. Willems op cit, 85
81 E. Riverso La teologia esistenzialistica di Karl Barth, (Naples 1955) 400
82 For a bibliography of the literature on Barth in Italian, cf, Problemi e Orientamenti vol I 658, and B. Gherardini La seconda riforma vol II 195-196
83 Cf, B. Willems op cit, 87; K. Barth Ad Limina Apostolorum 13; J. M. Alonso 'Karl Barth un criptocatólico?' Rivista Española de teología 17 (1957) 357-382; J. Alfaro 'Justificación Barthiana y justificación Catolica' Gregorianum 38 (1958)
84 G. Vagos 'Karl Barth, Professor e profeta' Brotéria 89 (1969) 3-17
85 H.V. Meynell op cit, Cf, P. Fransen loc cit, 42
86 C. O'Grady The Church in the Theology of Karl Barth (London 1968) 1-3; The Church in Catholic Theology 333-336
87 A.S. Nash:Introduction to Protestant Thought in the Twentieth Century (New York 1957) VII. The first book published in America on Barth is by W. Pauck Karl Barth. Prophet of a New Christianity? (New York 1931)
88 R. McAfee Brown Introduction to G. Casalis Portrait of Karl Barth XII
89 G. Weigel 'A Survey of Protestant Theology in Our Day' Proceedings of the Catholic Theological Society of America 11 (1950) 558
90 J.F. Andrews ed, Karl Barth (Saint Louis, Miss, 1969)
91 M.A. Fahey, Book review America 125 (1971) 18. We

should note that it also happened the other way around: S. Matczak <u>Karl Barth on God: The Knowledge of the Divine Existence</u> (New York 1962) was published in French in 1968.
92 K. Barth 'A Letter to the Author' H. Küng <u>Justification</u> XXI. Cf, H. Chavannes <u>op cit</u>, 306
93 P. Fransen <u>loc cit</u>, 47. Though most Catholic theologians have dealt with the main issues of Barth's teaching some have explored such topics as mariology: A.C. Cochrane 'The Theological Basis of Liturgical Devotion to Mary Re-examined' in <u>Marian Studies</u> 19 (1968) 49-69 (parallel between K. Barth and K. Rahner); G. Tait 'Karl Barth and the Virgin Mary' <u>Journal of Ecumenical Studies</u> 4 (1967) 406-425; K. Barth 'A Letter about Mariology' <u>Ad Limina Apostolorum</u> 59-62; Christian celibacy C. Starkloof 'Karl Barth on Christian Celibacy' <u>Review for Religious</u> 27 (1969) 1089-1096; marriage: O. Wond 'Le mariage dans la pensée de Karl Barth' <u>Istina</u> 15 (1970) 295-310
94 H. Bouillard 'Karl Barth et le Catholicisme' <u>loc cit</u>, 353
95 <u>Theology Today</u> 13 (1956-1957) 358-415
96 A. Dulles <u>loc cit</u>, 410
97 J.C. Bennett 'Karl Barth 1886-1968' <u>Christianity and Crisis</u> 28 (1968-1969) 326-328
98 H. Cox 'In Memory of Karl Barth' <u>Commonweal</u> 89 (1968-1969) 424-425
99 B. Willems 'Barth's abgebrokengesprek met Schleiermacher' <u>Tijdschrift voor theologie</u> 9 (1969) 2-10; C.F. Starklorr 'Schleiermacher and Barth on Religious Experience' <u>Revue de l'Université d'Ottawa</u> 39 (1969) 114-131
100 Cl. Geffre 'Declin ou renouveau de la theologie dogmatique' <u>Le Point théologique</u> Nr 1 (Paris 1971) 47-48
101 H. Urs von Balthasar <u>The Theology of Karl Barth</u> 19
102 K. Barth <u>Ad Limina Apostolorum</u> 27
103 Ibid, 20
104 Ibid, 17
105 Cf, A. Hasler 'Augustin Bea und Karl Barth in memoriam' <u>Theologisch praktische Quartalschrift</u> 117 (1969) 300, where is reproduced the very interesting letter of Karl Barth. For a local debate in reference to Barth: P. Hitz 'Actualité de Karl Barth' <u>Le Devoir</u> January 12 and 13 1970; with an answer by

a group of people involved in Catechetics: 'Réponse a
une critique' ibid, February 3 and 4 1970.
106 G. Vagos <u>loc cit</u>, 3
107 A. Dulles <u>loc cit</u>, 410

ARTHUR C. COCHRANE

The Karl Barth I Knew

What sort of a man was Karl Barth? Everyone knows and remembers another man from his own limited vantage point and from opportunities for personal contact with him and his work. I am sure that there are many who are better qualified to talk about Karl Barth and who have been more intimately acquainted with him than I. Certainly his son, Markus, could tell us much more about his father as a human being. For what relationship is closer than that of a father to a son, a son to a father? Perhaps wisely, perhaps for theological reasons, Markus chose instead to tell us something about the "current discussion on the political character of Karl Barth's theology." I rather think that this is what his father would want him to do.

Frankly I am troubled about talking about the man Karl Barth. I am not sure that the old gentleman would approve. You all will recall the tremendous impression which Grünewald's painting of Jesus made upon him -- of the finger of John the Baptist pointing to him on the Cross, of John who said: "I must decrease that he might increase." The fact is that one can only describe Karl Barth theologically, that is, in a broken, indirect, dialectical fashion, not because he was a theologian, but because he can be understood only in relation to Him who was "the object of his faith." The Karl Barth I knew was a man about whom, humanly speaking, one can know very little. Like Calvin but unlike Luther, Barth rarely wrote or talked about himself. When he did, as in the prefaces to the volumes of the Church Dogmatics, it was invariably in relation to his work in service of the Word of God. We know little about his religious experience, and nothing about his conversion. But somewhere along the line he must have come to the place where he no longer wanted to know himself or to be known "after the flesh" or "from a human point of view." From then on he deprecated any well-meant eulogies. He knew that the truth about himself is to be found in Christ. Consequently he consistently directed attention away from himself to Christ. As early as 1920 he noted "the surprisingly meager interest of the Bible in biography, in the development of its heroes. There is no gripping history of the youth and conversion of Jeremiah, no report of the edifying death of Paul. To the grief of our theological contemporaries there is above all no 'Life of Jesus.' What we hear of these men they never tell themselves; we do not read it in their 'life and letters.' The man of the Bible stands or falls with his task, his work."

So it is with Barth himself. If I may avail myself of christological analogies, I do not wish to give a docetic image of Barth, as if he were not a regular he-man. Nor do I wish to paint a Nestorian picture of Barth, as if his human nature could be understood apart from Jesus to whom he sought to bear witness.

One of my earliest and lasting impressions of Karl Barth is that he was a remarkably unreligious man. He once said: "I will not build a Christian home." This may sound strange, coming as it does from a man who had five children, one of whom (Markus) became a professor of New Testament, another (Christoph) a professor of the Old Testament. He wrote: "At the moment when religion becomes conscious of religion, when it becomes a psychologically and historically conceivable magnitude in the world, it falls away from its inner character, from its truth, to idols....The polemic of the Bible, unlike that of the religions, is directed not against the godless world but against the religious world, whether it worships under the auspices of Baal or of Jehovah."

Hence Barth's own polemic was directed against the religiosity of the 19th and 20th centuries. "Can a minister be saved?" he asked. "I would answer that with men this is impossible; but with God all things are possible. God may pluck us as a brand out of the fire. But so far as we know, there is no one who deserves the wrath of God more abundantly than the ministers." May I interject that this aspect of Barth is very relevant today when there seems to be a resurgence of experiential religion.

On the other hand, Barth was not a secularist or a wordling. In his latter years he showed considerable impatience with those who were writing about "the secular meaning of the Gospel", "the secular city" or about what "God is doing in the world." He had no desire "to take part in the discussions of the idiotic 'God is dead' movement, which on both sides of the Atlantic was showing itself to be the ultimate and fairest fruit of the glorious existential theology; and I had even less desire" he wrote, "to take part in the just as idiotic 'Confessional Movement'" -- a movement organized in Germany to oppose the former.[1] The truth is that Barth saw man, himself included, determined by an event beyond the dialectic of the secular and the religious. He saw both the publican and the Pharisee judged and pardoned by God in Jesus Christ.

Accordingly, the Karl Barth I knew was a humble man. We must be careful here. His humility was not an innate quality or virtue for which he could be praised or of which he could boast. He was humble because he had been <u>humbled</u> by God. At the celebration of his eightieth birthday in Basel, May 1966, he reminded those of us who attended that, though there might be great doctors, scientists and statesmen, there are only little theologians. In an article written September 1923 he declared: "The greatness of the fathers lay in their ability to see the gate definitely shut against all human greatness, and especially their own." During his visit to the United States in 1962 he was a guest in our home and met with a group of lay men and women who had been studying some of his works. One of the group, then a high school teacher, asked Dr. Barth to autograph a copy of his little book of sermons, <u>Deliverance to the Captives</u>. I remarked that a friend of mine had described that particular volume as "the brightest jewel in his crown." His reaction was swift and spontaneous: "I don't like that! I have no crown! I don't like that! I have no crown!" I tried to explain that my friend simply meant that this little book was the finest and best thing he had written. But I failed to pacify him.

At the same time Barth was not given to false modesty. He was well aware of his gifts and accomplishments, and of his place in history. For instance, in the foreward to the last and thirteenth volume of his great work, the <u>Church Dogmatics</u>, in which he attacked the doctrine and practice of baptism in the Roman Catholic, Lutheran and Reformed traditions, he wrote: "I foresee that with this book, which according to human judgment will be my last large publication, I will again stand in a certain loneliness in theological and Church circles such as I entered nearly fifty years ago, and that with it I am about to make a poor exit for myself! Be that as it may! The day will come when eventually in this matter also one will admit that I was right." One would err if one mistook such a statement for arrogance; it is the quiet confidence of a man who has bowed himself beneath the Scriptures in the face

THE KARL BARTH I KNEW

of a long entrenched tradition which he came to believe is contrary to the Word. If our Protestant Churches are again to be reformed, as the Roman Church is presently being renewed, not only this book but Barth's theology as a whole will need to be taken far more seriously than it has. The Karl Barth I knew is by no means a spent force. And the formation of the North American Karl Barth Society is evidence of this. Some scholars have been foolish enough to talk about a post-Barthian era when frankly I see little evidence that our generation has yet learned from him what a sermon is. Perhaps it was necessary for us to go through a period of existentialism and secularism in order to discover Barth's message.

Coupled with Barth's humility before God was a humility before his fellowmen. He knew how to listen to others before he spoke. I can confirm Professor T.F. Torrance's testimony that a visitor to Dr. Barth's home was plied with far more questions than he could put to his host. In his theological writings Barth is constantly putting questions to his contemporaries and to the Church fathers. He patiently and carefully weighed their arguments. He always maintained an immense respect for other scholars, even for those with whom he strongly disagreed. I recall that when I first visited Dr. Barth in 1936 I noted a picture of Friedrich Schleiermacher hanging on a wall -- the early 19th century theologian who has been described as "the father of modern liberal Protestantism." "Why not?" said Barth. "He was a good Christian." Barth never wanted to found a "Barthian" school of theology, much less a new church bearing his name. In 1963 he gave me a photograph of himself signed: "Karl Barth--kein Barthianer." (He was his own severest critic; hence he could make a drastic change in his view of christology and the sacraments from Vol. I to Vol. IV in the Church Dogmatics.) He simply wanted to be an active participant in the work of that community of teachers and learners which is the Church-- "the school of Christ." Though a member of the Reformed Church in Switzerland, he came to be recognized as an ecumenical theologian of the one, holy, catholic Church.

Was Barth a polemical or irenic theologian? If by polemics is meant plain-speaking, then Barth was polemical. He could address sharp rebukes to his closest followers. But he rarely spoke in anger or indulged in invectives. In all his writings I can think of only five instances. The most notorious, of course, was his No!, an answer to

THE KARL BARTH I KNEW

Emil Brunner's natural theology, with an "Angry Introduction." But let us recall the opening words of Barth's preface. "I am by nature a gentle being and averse to all unnecessary disputes. If anyone, faced with the fact that he is here reading a controversial treatise, should suggest that it would be so much nicer if theologians dwelt together in unity, he may rest assured that I heartily agree with him. Let me also impress upon him that, humanly and personally speaking, I have nothing against Emil Brunner....I should like nothing better than to walk together with him in concord, but in the Church we are concerned with truth, and today with an urgency such as probably has not been the case for centuries."

The time was 1934 when the persecuted Confessing Church was fighting for its life against the errors of the natural theology of the "German Christians" -- errors, by the way, which in other forms were and still are widespread throughout Christendom!

Barth's humility before God and man was the fruit of a knowledge not only of his own creatureliness but of his utter sinfulness. Once again we need to be careful. The awareness of his sin and guilt was not the result of a computation of his open and secret misdemeanors (of which, of course, he was not free) but of his knowledge of the revelation of the goodness of God in Jesus Christ. In the light of that revelation he knew that his best works, above all his piety, are as "a filthy rag." Wherefore, he could paradoxically affirm that sinful man, inasmuch as he remains God's creature, is altogether good, and that his sin is a denial of the goodness of his humanity. His love of the music of Mozart stemmed from his belief that Mozart, more than any Church father, had sounded the praises of the goodness of the Creator and his creation. I recall an unforgettable evening in 1958 when the two of us listened to all four of Mozart's Horn Concerti in his study after we had discussed theology for three hours! While most of his contemporaries--existentialists, novelists, artists, and composers--were giving expression to man's understanding of the emptiness, meaninglessness and hopelessness of existence, Barth was echoing the praise of the Book of Revelation: "Worthy art Thou, our Lord and God, to receive glory and honor and power, for Thou didst create all things, and by Thy will they existed and were created."

Accordingly Barth's dominant characteristics were his cheerfulness and humor. In the _Festschrift_ for his 70th birthday Heinrich Vogel contributed an article--not without a twinge of reproach--about "<u>Der lachende Barth</u>." Yes, Barth could laugh, and best of all at himself. Robert McAfee Brown has given us this delightful quotation. "The angels laugh at old Karl. They laugh at him because he tries to grasp the truth about God in a book of Dogmatics. They laugh at the fact that volume follows volume and each is thicker than the previous one. As they laugh, they say to one another, "Look! here he comes now with his little pushcart full of volumes of the Dogmatics! And they laugh about the men who write so much about Karl Barth instead of writing about the things he is trying to write about. Truly, the angels laugh."[2]

Barth's uncompromising opposition to natural theology, that is, to a theology based on a supposed revelation of God in nature, is well-known. But he could joke about that too. I remember a walk we had along the seashore at Aberdeen, Scotland, in 1936. I was plying him with questions about the first article of the Barmen Declaration and about the Gifford Lectures he was delivering on John Knox's Confession of Faith. For a moment he didn't hear me. He was lost in wonder, gazing out to sea. Then he said: "What did you say? <u>There</u> is the natural theology!"

His humour and perhaps also his theology is pointed up by another of his characteristics: his child-likeness. He would go down to the water's edge, moving forward and backward, to see if he would get his feet wet as the waves rolled in. Many years later a group of us were having breakfast with Dr. Barth at the Holiday Inn in Dubuque. In the adjoining booth was a young couple with a child of three or four years. Mimicking the sounds of a cow, a duck, a cat and a dog, he had the child in gales of laughter. He was as entranced with her as she was with him.

Barth's child-likeness and cheerfulness were expressions, I believe, of his simple trust in him who said: "Be of good cheer....I have overcome the world." Consequently he wrote that theology is "a peculiarly beautiful science. Indeed, we can confidently say that it is the most beautiful of all the sciences....The theologian who has no joy in his work is not a theologian at all. Sulky faces, morose thoughts and boring ways of speaking are intolerable in this science."[3] Theology was for him a joyful task because its object is the indescribably good news

THE KARL BARTH I KNEW

of "the beauty of the Lord our God" in the humiliation
and exaltation of Jesus Christ. And--in the words of
the poet, John Keats--"a thing of beauty is a joy forever;
its loveliness increases!"

NOTES

1 Ad Limina Apostolorum - An Appraisal of Vatican II.
   John Knox Press, Richmond 1968, p. 9.
2 Portrait of Karl Barth, George Casalis. Transl. with
   an Introduction by Robert McAfee Brown, New York 1963.
   p. 3.
3 Church Dogmatics II/1, p. 656.

THE CONTRIBUTORS

MARKUS BARTH, professor of New Testament and Ancient Church History at the University of Basel, formerly professor at Pittsburgh Theological Seminary.

ARTHUR C. COCHRANE, professor of Systematic Theology at Pittsburgh Theological Seminary.

EMILIEN LAMIRANDE, professeur d'histoire du Christianisme and chairman of the Department of Religious Studies at Université d'Ottawa.

PAUL L. LEHMANN, professor of Systematic Theology at Union Theological Seminary in Richmond, Virginia, formerly Charles A. Briggs professor of Systematic Theology at Union Theological Seminary, New York.

JOSEPH C. McLELLAND, professor of Philosophy of Religion at McGill University.

PAUL S. MINEAR, recently retired from his position of Winkley Professor of Biblical Theology at Yale University.

H. MARTIN RUMSCHEIDT, assistant professor of Historical Theology at the University of Windsor.

MICHAEL WYSCHOGROD, professor of Philosophy at Baruch College of the City University of New York.

www.ingramcontent.com/pod-product-compliance
Lightning Source LLC
Chambersburg PA
CBHW050825160426
43192CB00010B/1898